P9-CBS-249

The Edge Resume
and
Job Search Strategy

BY
Bill Corbin and Shelbi Wright

GRAPHICS BY
Jane Gard

PUBLISHED BY
UN Communications, Inc.
350 Gradle Drive
Carmel, Indiana 46032-7536

317-573-0234 • FAX 573-0239

Foreword

This book is about a successful job search. It includes discussion of some traditional fundamentals, but the heart of the Edge strategy is creativity. In the '90s, a successful campaign must be distinct. Within these pages are hundreds of ideas which you can use. Our ideas will spur your creativity...leading to a unique campaign, right for your goals and personality.

We invite you to forward samples and details of the campaign elements you utilize. Please correspond with

Bill Corbin
  or Shelbi Wright
The Edge
350 Gradle Drive
Carmel, IN 46032-7536

UN Communications, Inc.
350 Gradle Drive
Carmel, Indiana 46032-7536

317-573-0234 • FAX 573-0239

Copyright © 1993 by UN Communications, Inc. All rights reserved.
This book, or parts thereof, may not be reproduced in any form without permission.

Library of Congress Catalog Card No. 92-62613

ISBN: 0-9634373-0-5

First Printing.

Printed and bound in the United States of America.

"Retreating, hell! We're just attacking in a new direction!"

—

U.S. Marine General O.P. Smith, 1950,
completely surrounded by a North Korean army
when a reporter commented,
"It looks like your army is retreating, General."

Table of Contents

Intro...

There is little need to belabor the obvious: the '90s job market is very difficult.

There are too few jobs.

There are hundreds of companies in various stages of "restructuring"—a high-sounding concept which for many of us means, "They've eliminated my division, my department, and me."

Every year, a new batch of eager graduates pours out of high schools and colleges...and into direct competition for a variety of scarce jobs.

All in all, the situation is somewhere between discouraging and terrifying.

This book derives inspiration from the general quoted on the preceding page. The job market, like his battle position, seems bleak. Most of the conventional approaches to job searching, like his battle-plan to that point, aren't working. But General O.P. Smith, in the face of this adversity bellows, "Retreating, hell! We're just attacking in a new direction!" Let's adopt that spirit as we look at new approaches to energize your career search strategy.

"A new approach to the vital subject of securing interviews through your resume."

Some History...
and what it can teach us

Whether you are actively seeking a job or are considering the advisability of a career jump, you automatically "update your resume."

In most job searches, the resume is your equivalent of the carpenter's hammer: a critical, indispensable tool. A few brave souls knock out a new resume on a word processor and hope for the best. But most job seekers take the resume matter very seriously; spending time studying how-to books, consulting with literate friends, even working with professional resume writers.

Despite all these efforts, most resumes aren't working very well. The mailbox isn't full of positive responses. The phone isn't ringing. Obviously a weak job market makes things tough. But there is another vital reason why most resumes aren't working. Stated bluntly, there hasn't been a new idea regarding resume preparation in years—and the reality of Job Market '90s cries out for new ideas.

As is often the case, history provides lessons we can learn from...or ignore and be doomed to repeat.

"This should give Mr. Smedley enough people to choose from."

During the '70s and before, most of us simply typed our resume and made copies of it. Virtually all resumes were black ink on plain white paper. They weren't fancy but they seemed to work. Why? Because there were plenty of jobs.

In the early '80s, we hit a recession and the job market tightened. The resume experts correctly determined that "since your resume is in tougher competition, you should do things to make it stand out." Their analysis was correct; and their two primary pieces of advice were: (1) spend the money to have the resume professionally typeset, and (2) put it on ivory or gray paper.

While these were hardly bold technical advances, they did accomplish the purpose. Those seeking employees soon used the caliber of resume presentation as an important criterion for selecting candidates. Those seeking jobs soon realized that standards for a professional resume had risen, so the entire resume industry moved to a new level.

In the mid to late '80s, desktop publishing changed the resume game dramatically. Suddenly everyone could have a resume which appeared to be typeset—at modest cost and without the mystery of dealing with a printer who was typesetting by old-fashioned methods. Everyone had also learned that "my paper choice should be ivory or gray, not white." So we were back to the future—most resumes looked the same, certainly more attractive than the resumes of the '70s but still very similar to each other. Yet through the '80s these resumes worked nicely. Why? There were plenty of jobs.

"Someday you'll need to adopt these techniques to be competitive. Now you can adopt them to truly give yourself The Edge."

Today, hardly anyone's resume is working very well. Why? There aren't enough jobs. Your resume is again in extremely stiff competition. And, frankly, it looks just like everyone else's.

By elementary study of history, it would seem obvious that an important step is another visual upgrade. Yet the resume industry (book writers, resume services, etc.) has not made this important leap. The reason is simple enough. Desktop publishing and quick printing are deeply ingrained in both the knowledge base and the equipment base of the resume industry. So today's advisors have simply used the general appearance of resumes as a "given"—concentrating on issues such as writing style and "power phrases." Yet today's resume, when it sits in a pile 400 deep, is part of a literal "long gray (or maybe ivory) road" where it has very poor odds of being noticed.

With this book, the process of creating a striking, attention-grabbing resume will be made understandable. We'll then develop a creative multi-phase job search strategy which will further distinguish you from "the crowd." Someday you'll need to adopt these techniques to be competitive. Now you can adopt them to truly give yourself "The Edge."

A NOTE ON INVESTMENT

We'll cover a variety of ways to secure real value for dollars spent on your job search strategy. In general, however, creating a package which gives you a real Edge will cost more than typing your resume and making photocopies. You probably spent several years and tens of thousands of dollars to secure an education for Job #1. That you will need to spend a few bucks on your next job—especially in a miserable job market—makes sense.

Understanding The Edge...

The Edge concept includes a visually striking resume. It includes carefully chosen words which communicate far more effectively than does the typical resume. It includes a unique follow-up campaign. This book provides the information necessary for words, appearance and plan. More importantly, you must take a philosophical step. You will be attacking in a new direction, daring to be a bit different. The decision is made simpler by these powerful (if painful) truths:

- *In today's job market, your statistical odds of being considered for an attractive job are extremely low.*
- *An average job opening typically receives 200+ responses.*
- *An attractive job opening may receive a thousand.*
- *About 6 people will be interviewed.*
- *Therefore, unless your qualifications are so powerful that you are clearly in the top 1-3% of applicants, you won't even get an interview.*
- *So, you MUST take extraordinary steps to stand out in the pile of resumes.*

Thus far, we've discussed the Edge concept in the negative: the job market is tough, the statistics are lousy, you must attack in a new direction. While all of this is true, there is a much brighter side. This concept really works! It is based on logic and statistics; and once you understand the philosophy you will have a powerful new tool for your job search.

Let's assume we send out 100 resumes. Our resume looks different. It sounds different. It includes candor, perhaps humor, in unusual ways. When it arrives, the reader is forced to say, "This is NOT the typical applicant."

Now let's deal with the risk we're running. "But, what if people think my resume is too far out? What if they think all resumes are supposed to be black ink on gray or ivory paper? What if they don't like humor or unusual candor in a cover letter?"

Here's the key! We quickly grant that some people (who probably wear gray underwear under their gray suits) might question an unusual resume. In fact, let's make the very pessimistic assumption that 70 of our 100 recipients are not positive toward our approach. Note these KEY points:

- *REMEMBER—YOU ONLY NEED ONE JOB.*
- *All 100 recipients will react strongly to your resume. It will not be another gray brick on the long gray road.*
- *If 70 people reacted negatively, then 30 people reacted positively.*
- *You have an excellent chance of being noted, remembered and invited for an interview by those who react strongly in the positive.*

The absolute classic Edge resume (for which we claim no credit) was the guy who walked up and down Wall Street carrying his resume printed on a large sandwich board. Undoubtedly many of the people who saw him thought he was crazy. Dean Witter thought he was creative and courageous—and hired him.

An example of a unique resume is shown on page 18. However, as shown by the examples in Chapter 10, most of our resume concepts are not extreme. We are no less legible than conventional resumes. We are organized much like conventional resumes. But in the differences lie the opportunity for you to stand out. And it works!

The Edge philosophy also includes creative approaches to other aspects of the job search process. One of our associates, after failing on previous attempts to secure an interview with a target company, forwarded via UPS a life-size shoe. His note: "I've been trying unsuccessfully for months to get my foot in your door, so I decided to try another approach. I truly believe my qualifications are ideal for your company. A resume is enclosed..." He got the interview.

We'll cover a variety of approaches—most less extreme than mailing shoes—to reach our primary goal: standing out in the very tall stack of applications for attractive jobs.

The Jason Fritz Resume

Vol. 1 No. 1   301 Blake Drive, Fort Wayne, Indiana 46804   (219) 432-2327

Skip Moore Becomes WZZY Celebrity!

Since September 1990, the voice and personality of Jason Fritz have brought increasing fame and fortune to 98 WZZY in Randolph County, Indiana. Believing that anyone named Fritz would have to be good, WZZY immediately changed his name to Skip Moore and created a personality being followed by people of all ages throughout eastern Indiana and Western Ohio.

During his 40 hours of weekly airtime, Skip Moore hosts programs of his own

creation including Metal Marathon, The Best of The Dead and Monsters of Rock Tribute.

Moore fans also find him at local sports events and community activities where he conducts

Jason Fritz, aka Skip Moore, running the board.

a variety of live remotes. Moore's improvisational skills provide spontaneity and entertainment to his radio shows as well as his live DJ stints. His interviewing skills have been honed with one-on-ones including Gary Richrath of REO Speedwagon.

Even Fritz is a bit overwhelmed by Moore's popularity, "People are really following this guy," he exclaims, "I'm not sure I understand all the reasons, but it's good for business and a lot of fun!"

Fritz Ready To Move On

"Working at WZZY has been a fabulous experience," says Jason Fritz, "I've been able to work in every part of the business. But now it's time to put my skills to work in a larger market."

"I've proven I'm willing to tackle any job," Fritz continues, "and I would start wherever a new employer needs help. But I'm confident my programming and on-air skills will soon lead to a DJ position. I know I can build a profitable listenership for my station."

Details Of Fritz' Early Experience Revealed

It was no accident that Jason Fritz was ready to excel on and off the air at 98 WZZY. After serving as an intern at Rock 104 WXKE, Fort Wayne during the summer of 1987, Fritz knew he wanted to devote his working life to radio.

Because his work at WXKE was all behind the scenes he took every opportunity to learn how a radio station operates. "It was at that point that I began to assemble and build my own studio at home," says Fritz. He can now boast a complete and modern unit consisting of a 4-

track mixing board, compact disc players, tape decks, turntables and microphone.

"After I built and worked with my studio at home I was ready to work full-time for a radio station that could use my expertise." September 1990 was the first time that radio listeners picked up the voice of Jason Fritz, now known as Skip Moore.

While employed at 98 WZZY, Fritz was able to enroll in the Columbia School of Broadcasting in Indianapolis. He graduated in February 1992 with a degree in Radio Broadcasting.

Fritz Hits Pavement to Build Sales

Seeing the clear need for increased station revenues and desiring to add to his experience and income, Jason Fritz offered to become part of the WZZY sales team as well as an on-air personality. Mixing his various skills, Fritz secured management approval for several new programs, targeted advertisers for the new programming, then wrote, produced and sold the ads. A record number of new accounts were added for Fritz' Metal Marathon program.

"I want to be on the air," says Fritz, "but I believe in doing whatever needs to be done to help the station succeed. I realize, too, it's important to understand all parts of the business."

Fritz on the beat.

Using This Book...

This book covers a range of subjects beginning with your state of mind and ending with a successful interview. However, two truths are important:

1—There were many excellent reference books on the job search challenge before this one came along. Some of them cover specific topics in more depth than is possible here. Throughout this book, we list references which may provide additional help.

2—Depending upon your career status, some parts of this book will be more relevant to you than others. For example, our chapter on writing a resume draws heavily on traditional, proven concepts. If you are a first-time writer or your resume is badly outdated, this information will be helpful. If your word content is in good shape, you'll concentrate on the sections which cover approaches to gaining a competitive edge.

At virtually every stage in the book we present ideas aimed at allowing your application to stand out in heavy competition. Therefore, even if you have excellent skill in resume preparation, you will find our approaches give fresh ideas which can greatly improve your chances of gaining the attention you deserve.

In summary, our topics are:

- ***Your State of Mind*** *(Chapter 5): it is impossible to dynamically attack the job search if anxiety and fear are dominant emotions.*

- ***Introspection*** *(Chapter 6): you must know what kind of job you want—or are willing to accept—in order to decide how to conduct your search.*

- ***Finding the Opportunities*** *(Chapter 7): in a tough job market, you must find avenues other than the classifieds to find the right opportunities.*

- ***Marketing Your Skills*** *(Chapter 8): how your cover letter, resume and follow-up system should communicate with potential employers.*

- ***The Cover Letter*** *(Chapter 9): utilizing the most important opportunity to communicate your personal traits and values.*

- ***The Edge in Action*** *(Chapter 10): 30+ actual samples of Edge designs.*

- ***Make It a Campaign*** *(Chapter 11): completing the job search with appropriate follow-up communication. Some ideas are traditional; some very unique.*

- ***Use of Humor and Some Ideas Closer to the Edge*** *(Chapter 12): in some situations, it makes sense to dare to be very different. This chapter gives a variety of unique approaches.*

- ***Resume Writing*** *(Chapter 13): important concepts, most traditional, a few unique, for writing an effective resume. Valuable for first-time writers or usable as a guideline for critiquing your existing resume.*

- ***Interviewing*** *(Chapter 14): tips on preparing for and executing an effective interview.*

- ***Specific Action Steps*** *(Chapter 15): how to immediately put your knowledge to work.*

- ***Printing Specifications*** *(Appendix A): information which only a printer may understand—important in communicating your resume specifications.*

- ***Clip Art*** *(Appendix B):*

- ***The Edge Preprints*** *(Appendix C):*

Your State of Mind...

If you are fortunate, you are reading this book because you're considering a career change. You are comfortably situated at this time and are about to begin an orderly search for a better position. You are positive, confident, unhurried.

Or you may be on the other end of the spectrum. You were unexpectedly fired, laid off or otherwise "restructured." The clock is ticking on your savings account. You (not to mention your loved ones) are moving from anxiety toward out-and-out fear. Your confidence is embattled if not shot.

For some, the emotions of anxiety and fear are joined by an emotion very near grief. The career that I thought would be "for life," is unexpectedly over.

Some emotional turmoil is a predictable, natural part of the job search process. But it can do great violence to your ability to plan and execute an effective job search strategy. Your thinking can be muddled. Your cover letters and interviews can sound

"Thanks for participating in our profit improvement program, John!"

increasingly desperate. In general, you just aren't a very pretty picture in the competitive job market.

This book doesn't pretend to have answers to difficult emotional issues. But it does have the common sense to say this: If you are clearly embattled emotionally; if Roosevelt's famous "We have nothing to fear but fear itself" has taken on a very personal meaning, you must take the time to tackle this issue FIRST.

If this book could fulfill its goals perfectly, you might find new confidence and direction in the Edge job search strategy. However, you may need to patch a few leaks before setting sail. You may find answers in your religious faith; in support groups which increasingly address the needs of those in the job search project; in tapes or seminars aimed at self-confidence; or in the many books which specifically address this subject. Among the best known:

Bolles, Richard N., *The Three Boxes of Life, and How To Get Out of Them.* Ten Speed Press, Box 7123, Berkeley, CA 94707. 1978.

Crystal, John C., and Bolles, Richard N., *Where Do I Go From Here With My Life?* Ten Speed Press, Box 7123, Berkeley, CA 94707. 1974.

DuBrin, Andrew, *Your Own Worst Enemy: How To Overcome Career Self-Sabotage.* AMACOM, 135 W. 50th Street, New York, NY 10020. 1992.

Sinetar, Marsha, *Do What You Love, The Money Will Follow.* Dell Publishing, 666 Fifth Ave., New York, NY 10103. 1989, 1987.

> **"If Roosevelt's famous 'We have nothing to fear but fear itself' has taken on a very personal meaning, you must take the time to tackle this issue FIRST."**

6

Introspection...

what kind of job do I want anyway?

By definition, introspection is a very personal process. There are no right answers. It's even difficult to find the right questions.

But the process is absolutely crucial. If you are "successful" in finding a job, but spend the next several years being miserable about its requirements, income or location, the job search certainly doesn't deserve to be called successful.

More positively, introspection might lead to a broader definition of potential jobs; for example, veterans of traditional companies might consider opportunities in the non-profit sector or vice versa; or veterans of a particular industry might find their skills easily transferable to another industry.

"I know you'd love to be a professional golfer John, but you haven't shot under 90 all year."

First ask yourself broad questions such as:

- What are my skills?
- What do I like to do?
- What do I hate to do?
- What jobs fit my skills and desires?
- What are my practical needs for cash?
- How much adjustment am I willing to make to redirect my career?
  —Change of responsibility?
  —Development of new skills?
  —Reduction of income?
  —Relocation?
- Are my loved ones comfortable with my direction?

At a more detailed level factor in:

- Bonuses? Stock Options? Perks?
- Leadership? Management or staff member? Authority or subordinate?
- Prestige? Important title? Impressive company?
- Variety? Many or few responsibilities? Constantly changing or never changing functions? Similar days or different days?
- Advancement opportunities?
- Challenge on the job? Or familiarity with what you do and what's expected of you?
- On-the-job learning and training?
- Independence?
- Job security? Or a volatile position, department or company?
- Easy commute? How long am I willing to travel to get to work?
- Flexible hours? Structured hours?
- Interaction with co-workers? Prefer to work with others or alone?
- Contribution to society? Directly or indirectly?
- Long-term or short-term employment? Retire with this company or part of your corporate ladder?
- Company size? Large or small? Local, national, international?
- Personal office? Amenities?
- Travel? How many days out of the year? Daily, weekly, monthly? Locally, nationally, internationally?

At the very least, you should list those factors which are important to you and attempt to compare the list to the jobs being considered.

Several excellent books help guide you through this process. Among them:

Bolles, Richard Nelson, *What Color Is Your Parachute? A Practical Manual for Job-Hunters & Career-Changers.* Ten Speed Press, P.O. Box 7123, Berkeley, CA 94707. 1991.

Miller, Arthur F. and Mattson, Ralph T., *The Truth About You: Discover What You Should Be Doing With Your Life.* Ten Speed Press, P.O. Box 7123, Berkeley, CA 94707. 1989, 1977.

Tieger, Paul D. and Barron-Tieger, Barbara, *Do What You Are: Discover The Perfect Career For You Through The Secrets Of Personality Type.* Little, Brown and Company, Canada. 1992.

In addition, a computer program entitled SIGI PLUS has been developed for college students as well as seasoned professionals. This detailed program helps prioritize your values and skills then lists careers that correspond to your priorities. The program is distributed primarily through colleges and high schools but may be available in some public libraries.

If "human guidance" is helpful in your evaluation process, consider a career counselor. Effectiveness of professional counselors varies widely, so it is probably best to work with someone referred by an associate.

A host of self-help groups have sprung up around the country, providing an opportunity for introspection via honest dialogue with others facing the same career challenges.

"At the very least, you should list those factors which are important to you and attempt to compare the list to the jobs being considered."

Finding Opportunity

In a perfect world, you would pour a cup of coffee, grab your red pen, peruse the Sunday classified section, and find the job which perfectly matches your skills and goals. Not likely in the '90s. This chapter covers AGGRESSIVE seeking of opportunity—the kind of action which is a virtual necessity in a difficult job market.

Certainly the classifieds are a source of opportunities. Study the local ads. Study the ads in cities to which you'd move for the right opportunity. Fire off your Edge marketing salvo (cover letter, resume, and follow-up material) and hope for the best. But rather than simply sitting, waiting and hoping, dive aggressively into other search avenues.

There are two important reasons for aggressive alternative action:

1. It's your best statistical chance.

2. Those relying strictly on classified ads often experience mounting frustration, anxiety and fear. As time passes without the hoped for response, these emotions can lead to an attitude of helplessness and defeat. If you're in high-gear, making calls, writing letters and researching companies inside and outside your industry, the positive action gives you critical forward momentum.

First be aware that you are in a very dynamic job market. In fact, some opportunities are created by the difficulties of a struggling economy.

"Rather than simply sitting, waiting and hoping, dive aggressively into other search avenues."

Somewhere out there:
- An irate Board of Directors will fire the CEO and most of his fellow incompetents.
- Several embattled CEOs, hoping to avoid being fired by their Board of Directors, will fire incompetent staff members.
- Several embattled staff members, hoping to avoid being fired by the CEO, will fire incompetent subordinates.
- Several people in your job category will die or become incapacitated.
- Aggressive young companies will launch new divisions or product lines.
- Successful entrepreneurs will realize they can no longer do it alone and will start building a management staff.
- Non-profit organizations will receive the grant they needed to start a new endeavor.

The difficulty, of course, is knowing who will have these opportunities and when. Your strategy must be...
- Aggressive study,
- Timely communication of your skills, preferably in advance of the moment opportunity actually occurs,
- Continuing follow-up as opportunity does occur.

Mentally, you must be in constant research mode. Devour the local news, major newspapers and any business-oriented publications which carry relevant information. Read every item with the mindset: "What does this mean in terms of job opportunity?" As you zero in on specific job opportunities, make every effort to get closer to that organization.
- Study and organize every available piece of information you can find on the company (see box for guidelines).
- If you have acquaintances who work there, pump them for any relevant information and contact names.
- If possible, arrange an informational interview with one of their managers (discussed on page 30).
- Prepare a cover letter which demonstrates your unusual degree of interest and knowledge.
- Forward your resume, hand-carried by an acquaintance if possible, to the key decision-maker.

Another vital action step involves that overworked buzzword of the '90s: "networking."

In addition to communicating your availability to friends, neighbors and clergy, it's possible to network creatively.

- Communicate with every professional contact on your Rolodex wheel.
- Ask your relatives and close friends for access to their network of friends, business associates and contacts.
- Become active in local clubs or organizations, especially those geared toward your profession of choice or interest.
- Reconnect with old high school or college friends.
- If applicable, reconnect with former teachers or even administrators.

Some Questions To Guide You In Company Research

1. How old is the organization?
2. What are its products/services?
3. Where are its plants, offices or stores located?
4. Has the organization shown substantial and consistent growth?
5. What is its financial condition?
6. What are its new products/services?
7. Are there any plans for expansion?
8. Who are the company's primary customers?
9. Who are the organization's major competitors?
10. How does the organization rank in the industry?
11. What were the company's gross sales last year?
12. What is the organization's public image? Has it been in the media lately?
13. To what degree is the organization committed to solving community problems? How has it contributed to the community?
14. Does the company have excessive employee turnover or other unusual organizational traits?
15. How centralized is the organizational structure? Do subordinates participate in decision-making activities?

Among the sources: Standard and Poor's, The Thomas Register, The National Job Bank, The Directory of Directories

Communication with your network should be both verbal and written. A phone call may be useful in re-establishing contact, but verbal contact unsupported by written contact tends toward:

"Pete, John Miller here...you remember me...(fill in the years)...hey, Pete, I'm as they say 'between engagements'...if you hear of anything that I might fit into, let me know, OK?"

"Hey, sure, John—and great to hear from ya after all these years...bye."

Pete, with no notes and only a temporary warm glow, is almost certain to forget the entire discussion by tomorrow morning. However, if he receives a supporting cover letter and resume within a couple of days, the odds of action increase dramatically.

Remember to communicate the proper role of your network. Pete does not need to be able to call you back in three days and say, "John, good news, you start next Monday at Acme Electronics." In fact, the burden of "finding you a job" will paralyze most people. You're simply asking that they advise you of:

- Openings they become aware of;
- High potential situations they may know of;
- Other networking sources for you to contact;

If they can "put in a good word for you," it's great. If you can mention their names as referrals, that helps too. But, in general, you're simply asking for help in locating opportunities—not for help in actually landing the job.

Other Avenues of Opportunity

INFORMATIONAL INTERVIEWS

The informational interview can be an excellent door opener. You are asking for perhaps 20 minutes of a manager's time to learn more about his/her industry, company and job position. Some people will turn down requests for interviews, but a sizable percentage will be flattered by the request and will enjoy the opportunity to speak as an expert. From your standpoint, there are three major benefits:

- You will add to your knowledge bank regarding companies you're interested in.
- You will gain valuable experience regarding the interviewing process—in effect from the other side of the desk.
- You might make the kind of contact and favorable impression which can lead directly to a job.

Most effective in arranging the interview is direct intervention by part of your network. If this isn't feasible, forward a letter explaining your interest and follow-up by phone. A well-prepared list of questions and attentive note-taking are important parts of presenting a professional image. These questions are typical:

1. What are your responsibilities and duties? Can you give me some examples of your responsibilities and duties?
2. What happens during a typical work day in your position?
3. What do you like about your job?
4. What do you dislike about your job?
5. What do you like about this industry?
6. What do you dislike about this industry?
7. How did you get into this field?
8. What skills, qualifications and other credentials are essential to be hired for this position?
9. What courses should I take, books should I read, or other experiences should I gain to prepare more fully for this type of work?
10. What type of training is available in this industry?
11. What advancement opportunities exist?
12. What is the salary range for employees in this field and how do the salaries progress over the longer term?
13. What are the future trends in this field?
14. Who are your major competitors?
15. What sets your organization apart from your competitors?
16. What personal characteristics do you perceive to be critical to succeed in this field?
17. What is the typical career path for someone in this field?

The atmosphere should be relaxed with no clear angling for a position. However, it is possible that the impression made during the interview will lead to opportunity within that company.

One Edge associate conducted extensive library research on pharmaceutical companies. She contacted the sales managers of the top five firms who were selling in her city. All five agreed to spend twenty minutes answering her questions and were impressed enough with her knowledge of their field that she received three opportunities to interview within the companies.

SMALL BUSINESS OBSERVATIONAL VISITS

A variation on the informational interview is possible in some small companies. Ask the CEO for the opportunity to observe the operation and to make a report on your findings. If your insights and recommendations are impressive, you have an improved chance for any job openings.

TRADE ASSOCIATIONS AND THEIR PUBLICATIONS

Your library trips can yield the names of trade associations in your industry of preference. Securing copies of association publications can provide valuable information on trends within specific companies. Every industry has several specialty magazines carrying stories indicating who is growing, launching new divisions and closing.

BROADEN YOUR SCOPE

A recent Edge client successfully jumped into an operations position in a national floral company. His previ-

"Many hirers are aware that skills are transferable among industries and are willing to consider those making a sizable career jump."

ous stops had included operations positions in an electric motor company, a record/tape distribution company, and a national restaurant chain. Many hirers are aware that skills are transferable among industries and are willing to consider those making a sizable career jump.

EMPLOYMENT AGENCIES AND EXECUTIVE SEARCH FIRMS

The Yellow Pages are a useful starting point regarding agencies specializing in locating jobs in your profession. However, be aware that companies vary significantly in effectiveness—so make every effort to research the success ratio of prospective firms. Most search firms derive their income from the employers. If the fee is paid by the job seeker, be very aware of all costs and the benefits which are promised. A slow job market probably means that search companies are heavy-laden with clients seeking employment. The going will be slow, so be patient and actively explore other opportunities.

TEMPORARY AGENCIES

If you are currently unemployed, temporary agencies may provide income, momentum, and an avenue inside companies of choice. (Again, the Yellow Pages are a source, but you should research agency effectiveness).

"You know, Mary, I'm afraid John may be carrying this networking idea too far."

CONSULTING AND PROJECT WORK

An alternative to interim employment is consulting or project work. Your research or your network may suggest opportunities to help companies who are expanding or companies who are struggling. You offer to join their team on an independent contractor basis. You sell the benefit that they can complete key projects without committing to a full-time hire. While on the job, you can determine if the company is your kind of place in a career sense. If so, you can attempt to parlay the opportunity into a position.

One Edge associate, out of a job but still enjoying adequate severance resources, made a company this unusual offer: "I know you need to implement a new employee evaluation system. I'll undertake the project on this basis: If I handle it to your full satisfaction, you'll pay me a fair price. If not, you'll pay me nothing." His approach secured a consulting contract; and, although he had originally hoped for a full-time job offer, he learned he was good enough at consulting to make his consulting practice a full-time career.

CHAPTER 8

Marketing...

The job search process involves not one but two levels of marketing. It might occasionally happen that a brilliantly crafted cover letter along with a "perfect" resume arrives, the recipient says, "Eureka, I have found him/her!" and you're in. But, it's not likely. The probable reality:

LEVEL ONE:

- A basketful of resumes and cover letters are being reviewed;
- A handful survive initial screening;
- That handful is further screened to select a few people to be interviewed;
- If you're still in the running, your LEVEL ONE selling job was a success...and greatly improving your LEVEL ONE odds is the primary purpose of this book.

LEVEL TWO:

You chat, smile, dance, sing (and never let 'em see you sweat) in order to convince the interviewer that you're the best applicant.

Chapter 14 covers some ideas and references on the interviewing process.

2.
Get the Job

1.
Get the Interview

Good marketing certainly involves a predetermined set of steps. For example:

- Research as much as possible.
- Write a personal cover letter utilizing and demonstrating knowledge gained during research.
- Forward the cover letter with a powerful, visually striking resume.
- Follow-up by phone in a few days.
- Follow-up with a clever card in a few more days.
- Follow-up again by phone.

However, flexibility can be equally important. Examples of flexibility include possibilities such as:

- Your research shows that the resume will go directly to the hiring manager (vs. a Human Resources manager). You are able to learn something about the manager (favorite sports team, college attended, sense of humor, appreciation of blunt, straightforward talk). You tailor your cover letter to utilize that knowledge.
- Your research shows that the resume will be routed through Human Resources. Therefore an additional level of marketing is involved to survive the first cut in Human Resources. Your cover letter stresses the kinds of qualifications and personal traits which clearly make you the kind of person the hiring manager will want to consider. If it's possible to learn enough about the company's hiring system, consider two cover letters—one to the initial screener and one to the hirer. Typically a phone call will secure enough information to guide your approach.

"Good marketing certainly involves a predetermined set of steps...however, flexibility can be equally important."

Often, flexibility includes multiple versions of your resume. One of our associates recently survived the screening of 1200 resumes to become one of 10 interviewees. His commentary is loaded with wisdom: "First a Human Resource clerk scanned the resumes for the best 200. These went to the Human Resource manager who forwarded 30 to the hiring executive. I figured the time spent in first screening might be 30 seconds. So I loaded the cover letter with reasons my qualifications matched their requirements. I used a version of my resume which emphasized the skills they were seeking. I'm pretty sure the cover letter alone got me through the first screening. Then the strong resume led to an interview."

USING THE EDGE PHILOSOPHY

Visualize a continuum between these two extremes:

(1) You hear about a job for which you're perfectly qualified. You not only fit the educational and professional requirements, you were recently publicized in a widely read worldwide industry magazine as "_____(job title)_____ of the Year."

(2) You are determined to make a major career change. You must convince someone that, despite zero apparent qualifications, you are a capable, bright and quick study, and will make him very happy he was willing to take a chance on you.

In point of fact, every situation you look into will fall somewhere on this continuum, and your marketing approach MUST vary to reflect reality. Our

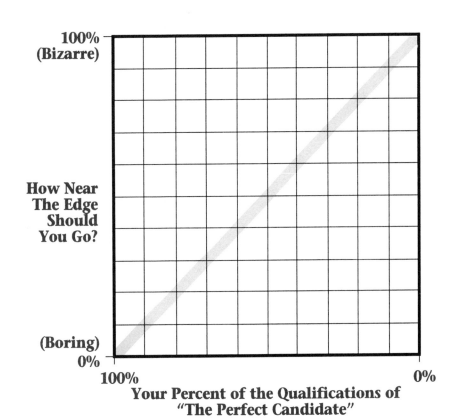

100%
(Bizarre)

How Near
The Edge
Should
You Go?

(Boring)
0%

100%   0%

**Your Percent of the Qualifications of
"The Perfect Candidate"**

theoretically perfectly qualified candidate probably writes a two paragraph letter announcing "I am willing to join your firm. My requirements are..." A classic example of overcoming poor qualifications is a graphic artist who wrote: "I know you'll see resumes with more formal job experience than I've had. But I also know I'm capable of quickly learning the job and accomplishing more than you presently think possible. To demonstrate my confidence, I'm willing to start at any wage you offer (including minimum) while I prove what I can do." She got the interview, got the job (at a reasonable starting wage), and accomplished everything she promised.

Let's pause to examine this woman's approach as an example of Edge philosophy. Critics say, "You should never suggest you're less than fully qualified. You surely shouldn't say you're willing to work for a pittance." The critics overlook this critical truth. The applicant was not as qualified as other applicants. Even casual comparison of her resume showed her to have less experience than competitors. Based purely on the information on her resume, she had ZERO CHANCE of being hired. Therefore, she had nothing to lose and everything to gain by a unique approach.

You must realistically assess your odds of securing the position. The worse that your apparent odds are, the further toward "The Edge" you must move to have any practical chance of surviving the screening process. Our example of forwarding an actual shoe was inspired by Edge analysis. "I've not succeeded in breaking through to this company. I surely don't have much to lose by trying something unique. Let's give it a try."

On the other hand, if your qualifications are very strong, your goal should simply be a powerful, well-organized resume package which stands out graphically: clearly superior to the rest of the stack, but otherwise basically traditional.

The Cover Letter...

In achieving an Edge, your cover letter is at least as important as the resume.

It should be:

- Striking in appearance, with the same design theme as the resume.
- Fully professional in appearance; carefully proofread to avoid grammatical errors, spelling errors or typos.
- Personalized to a name, not "To Whom It May Concern."
- Consistent with your marketing strategy:
  — Experience-oriented if your experience is strong.
  — More unique and more values-oriented if your experience is not likely to be competitive with other applicants.

"If you have the right technology...you'll be amazed how much more dynamic your search process can be."

Three preliminary topics are important:

TECHNOLOGY

It's crucial to have access to modern word processing technology to process cover letters. This allows the addressee to be easily personalized and your "base letter" to be edited to include information specific to the recipient. Print quality should be excellent. Laser quality is best; excellent dot matrix (NLQ-near letter quality) may be acceptable, but ask your most critical friend if it looks fully professional.

In general, strive to make "smooth, easy communication" a positive tool in your job search. Too often people fail to get off an important letter simply because it's a hassle to get it typed. We've heard admissions that "I didn't mail that letter because I didn't have a stamp." If you have the computer technology—buy or rent if unavailable—and all the supplies which make communication easy, you'll be amazed how much more dynamic your search process can be.

THE ADDRESSEE

Even at considerable cost of library time or long-distance phone charges, invest in real names. A cover letter addressed to PERSONNEL MANAGER or HUMAN RESOURCES COORDINATOR or TO WHOM IT MAY CONCERN has virtually no chance of being competitive.

THE QUESTION OF THE ENVELOPE

There are two issues:

Size: The two envelope choices are #10, the standard business size which involves tri-folding your contents; and 9x12 catalog envelopes, which allow the contents to be inserted without folding.

Cost of the two alternatives may be surprisingly similar. If you select a #10 which matches the resume, cost of this premium stock is relatively high. 9x12's are typically plain white paper—larger but similar in cost.

Under current postage regulations, there is a premium to mail the larger size, probably about $.10 per mailing.

By the fact that #10 stock can match your letter and resume stock, it's possible to create a dramatically designed matching set.

The only argument for the 9x12 is that your resume remains flat, therefore slightly more attractive and easier to file. There's little indication that this benefit is compelling at the reader level; so, while it's a matter of taste, we lean toward the matching #10.

Paper Stock: Premium envelopes which match your resume paper are expensive versus purchasing plain white #10's at the discount office supply store—probably under a penny each. Some argue that the envelope is ripped and pitched immediately; therefore the cheapie is acceptable. While this position is arguable, it is clearly not consistent with the Edge concept of creating a truly standout resume package. We conclude that a matching envelope is worth the investment.

The Cover Letter:

At its most basic, this letter covers:

- How you became aware of the opportunity;
- What you know about the company and the opportunity;
- Your personal traits which make it clear you should be considered for the position;
- A direct request for an interview.

Chapter 10 includes four complete cover letters. In several respects, the sample on page 53 represents the ideal cover letter. The hiring company had listed the qualifications they were seeking. The applicant had strong enough experience to confidently fill each need. The cover letter became a virtual "check list" and was successful. This approach is usable unless you are so clearly stretching your relevant experiences that the recipient begins chuckling as he "deep sixes" your package.

If you do not have knowledge of the specific job or qualifications a company is seeking, utilize your research to tie likely needs to your skills. For example:

"Since profit margins in the steel industry have been squeezed by foreign competition, it's clear that aggressive programs to cut cost and raise efficiency are vital. In the last three years, I have reduced cost of goods sold by 4% through a combination of labor efficiencies and creative purchasing. I am confident my experience fits perfectly with your need and look forward to discussing this job opportunity with you."

• • • • • • • • • • • • • • • • • •

"A mutual acquaintance, John Smith, filled me in on the competitive challenge you face since ABC Corporation moved into your primary marketplace. The possibility of significant loss of established customers is a threat to be addressed aggressively. Between 1987 and 1991, I served as Marketing Director in my company's Midwest region. We faced new competition from XYZ Corporation, and implemented a powerful series of counterattacks which resulted in a 2% increase in market share. I am confident..."

• • • • • • • • • • • • • • • • • •

"While studying your company in The Wall Street Journal and several trade publications, I became aware of the difficult strike situation faced last year. Of course, the aftermath is always a period filled with conflict and morale difficulties. In 1988, I served as Corporate Communications Director where I was directly responsible for rebuilding morale through a series of creative communication vehicles. I am confident..."

If qualifications do not clearly meet the company's needs, you are faced with an interesting dilemma: fib or find another way.

Many resume writers resort to creative puffery. One writer admitted his phrase "worked closely with top management on evaluation of national ad campaign" was inspired by an elevator ride when the CEO casually asked what he thought of a new ad. Readers of resumes know the resume is probably puffed. ("If this person was really this good, she'd be president of her company instead of looking for a job.")

The Edge concept offers an important alternative: Candor coupled with expression of positive personal VALUES can overcome shortcomings in resume qualifications.

Two crucial considerations must be understood:

- Every experienced hirer knows that real con artists can write good resumes. These people, while qualified on paper, may be nasty, lazy, insolent to superiors, brutal to subordinates, drunkards, liars or thieves. While we exaggerate a bit (for comic relief), it remains true: technical job skills do not assure a good employee; good employees must also have good personal values. Therefore, in the expression of VALUES, you have an opportunity to overcome some resume shortcomings.

- Speaking frankly, it's important to be sure you have good values before you communicate them in your cover letter. If necessary, examine those values such as your work ethic, your ability to work smoothly with people and your ability to handle stress without losing your sense of humor. False communication regarding values will not ring true—and the person hired as a hard worker will be fired as soon as he turns out to be a 3:30 p.m. golf junkie.

"Marge, do we have any openings for guys who can leap tall buildings in a single bound?"

Here are some examples of values communication which can work in a cover letter:

"I'm well aware that in today's job market, you'll find people with more years of experience than I've had. You won't find anyone willing to learn faster or work harder. I'll study and take classes on my own time. And I'll succeed in this job through a level of hard work and dedication to excellence which will serve as a positive example for other employees."

• •

"Review of my resume will show I'm moving from a stagnant industry into your far more dynamic field. Therefore, my qualifications may not seem to directly apply. However, please be aware that I have directly managed a staff of ___, been accountable for a budget of ___, and have demonstrated my versatility through successful stints as _____, _____, and _____. I study hard and learn quickly. On the job I ride hard, shoot straight, and never quit until the job is done. I'm confident you'll find my performance consistent with the commitment to excellence your company has made."

• •

"OK, I need a little extra help here. When you see my resume, you're going to say, "Hey, this guy is too young, too green, or too something to be considered." WAIT! STOP! DON'T PUT ME ON THE BOTTOM OF THE STACK! You'll be happy you gave me a little extra consideration.

All my life I've succeeded by setting high goals then working as hard as it takes to achieve them. I work extremely well with people. I learn fast and communicate well. I even accept criticism gracefully and take whatever steps are needed to fix what's wrong.

Give me an interview. You won't be sorry!"

In some cases, particularly when applying for high-level leadership positions, communication of values can be as important as communication of experience. For example:

"As an applicant for your vital leadership position, I'd like to step outside 'resume mode' for just a minute. I'm sure my job qualifications are competitive. I've been 'down the road' in the necessary areas of marketing, finance, manufacturing and human resources. But I feel strongly that effective leadership has more to do with values than the length of a resume. I lead by example; by demonstrated hard work and commitment to excellence. I build an effective team the same way successful coaches build teams. We build pride through performance; and performance through relentless execution of the fundamentals of our business. From all I know about your company, we share the same goals and the same commitment to excellence. I look forward..."

Humor:

A strange void in the resume field is humor. A recent study of "bosses" determined that sense of humor is viewed as one of the most important single traits of employees. Yet humor is vary rare and, used carefully, is a clear opportunity to execute the Edge philosophy. Why not a clever quote at the bottom of your cover letter or an appropriate cartoon printed on your envelope? We'll cover more on humor in Chapter 12.

❝*In some cases...communication of values can be as important as communicaton of experience.*❞

45

The Edge In Action

The following 30 pages represent samples of Edge resumes and cover letters "in living color." The contents of each page have been "fictionalized to protect the innocent," but the words and formats may be helpful as you begin to write your resume.

We suggest use of this section in three ways:

- A quick thumb-through to gain an overall impression of the kinds of techniques which create an Edge resume.
- A more detailed search for approaches which fit your personal style and career need.
- Development and execution of the design with your printer or resume consultant.

This section can be used to stimulate your creative processes, leading to your own unique design. Or you may simply copy the ideas presented here.

Cost of executing these ideas varies significantly. Some of the resumes can be accomplished with a desktop publisher and a fine quality copier. Others require the expertise of a strong commercial printer. Appendix A discusses the cost issues as well as the technical specifications for preparing each design.

You may want to study Appendix A carefully. Or you may want to skim the cost information for an affordable design and let your printer wade through the technical details.

In Appendix B we present various "clip art" which may be useful in preparing your resume.

Appendix C discusses an approach to developing a sophisticated design at relatively low cost. The "preprinted shell" is paper which already includes the borders, foil or diecuts which make many designs unique. You can secure these "shells" from The Edge or other sources and simply copy your resume onto the shell by conventional printing methods.

January 15, 1992

Ms. Elizabeth Brooks
Senior Vice President
Corporate Communications
American United Life
One American Square
Indianapolis, IN 46204

Dear Ms. Brooks:

If there's a piece missing from your organizational puzzle, I believe my background and skills will fit perfectly with your needs.

Review of my resume will indicate my knowledge in the fields of public relations, marketing and mass media. Hopefully, my somewhat unique resume design will indicate the kind of initiative and creativity so important in the field of communications.

I am also aware of the growing role of public relations in the insurance industry and am excited about utilizing my energy and talent in this important arena. Should you agree that my skills match the requirements for a position in your Corporate Communications Department, I will look forward to the opportunity to meet with you to discuss specifics.

Thank you for your time and consideration. I look forward to hearing from you soon.

Sincerely,

Susan Miller
Susan Miller

SUSAN L. MILLER
7450 North College Avenue
Indianapolis, Indiana 46260
(317) 255-1870

QUALIFICATIONS
- Conductor of more than 100 seminars on communications and marketing topics
- Effective problem solver using excellent written and verbal communication skills
- 10 years experience as a marketing and public relations manager
- Proficient with computers including word processing, database, spreadsheet, desktop publishing and graphics software
- Co-author, editor and designer of *Layout and Editing Techniques for Beginners*

EXPERIENCE
6/78–Present Owner and Communications Consultant
Graphics Publications, Indianapolis, Indiana

Write, publish and market publications on the subject of communicating through print medium. Advise organizations about establishing and conducting internal and external communications programs as well as dealing with problems related to those programs. Create workshops and seminars presented to professional communicators.

2/88–3/91 Corporate Communications Director
Ellis, Russell & Associates, Inc., Indianapolis, Indiana

Provided communications, editing, desktop publishing, marketing and printing support to corporate headquarters and 12 regional offices of the United States' largest insurance brokerage firm. Published quarterly newsletter mailed to more than 3,000 clients and potential clients. Managed and maintained newsletter mailing list database. Produced status reports for clients; monthly and quarterly sales and production reports and charts; marketing and training aids; brochures; booklets; and manuals.

2/85–1/88 Marketing Manager
American Financial Services, Indianapolis, Indiana

Conducted market research, developed marketing strategies and set up effective working relationships with a major local bank and a data services company. Recruited and trained sales staff. Designed and produced marketing collateral materials and other sales aids. Produced company training videotapes.

11/80–1/85 Public Relations Director
Indianapolis Developmental Center, Indianapolis, Indiana

Developed and administered all internal and external communications programs for Indiana's largest facility serving the mentally and physically handicapped. Directed community education, media relations, printing and audio-visual operations. Evaluated and analyzed programs and resources available in four departments while providing operational guidance and supervision to staff. Edited press releases, annual reports, personnel recruiting materials.

EDUCATION
DePauw University, Greencastle, Indiana
Bachelor of Arts in Communications, 1978

March 7, 1992

Mr. Brent Starr
President
Atlantic Richfield Company
515 South Flower Street
Los Angeles, CA 90071

Dear Mr. Starr:

Your advertisement in the Indianapolis Star for Vice President-Finance was of great interest to me. I believe there is an excellent match between your requirements and my qualifications:

YOUR REQUIREMENTS	MY QUALIFICATIONS
1. Minimum of 5-7 years experience in financial analysis and management.	1. I have 11 years experience as a financial analyst. During six of these years I have supervised the work of 7 other analysts.
2. Budget preparation experience a plus.	2. Budget preparation has always been part of my responsibility. I have successfully managed budgets in excess of $50 million.
3. MBA in Finance required.	3. In 1984, I obtained my MBA in Corporate Finance & Quantitative Analysis from Indiana University.
4. Ability to develop and implement change and improvements.	4. This has always been a strong area of expertise including two complete restructuring of systems which were being computerized.

A personal interview will give both of us an opportunity to explore mutual interests. Thank you for your consideration and I look forward to hearing from you soon.

Sincerely,

Andrew Freeman

Andrew Freeman

Andrew Freeman

7181 North Cooper Street
Indianapolis, Indiana 46220
(317) 844-8909

SUMMARY OF QUALIFICATIONS
- Successfully managed budgets in excess of $5 million.
- Experienced in developing short- and long-term financial business planning.
- Effective problem solver using excellent written and verbal communication skills.
- Demonstrated expertise in operations consolidation and divestiture.

EMPLOYMENT HISTORY

March 1975–Present
Shell Oil Corporation, *Indianapolis, Indiana*

Supervisor, Financial Analyst   **July 1985–Present**
- Manage, train and develop seven MBA analysts responsible for systems development and financial planning to optimize return on investment, evaluate long range resource requirements and organize management sciences activities.
- Consolidated all economic planning within controller's portfolio by implementing departmental reorganization.
- Initiated proposal to optimize manufacturing facility which increased productivity 175%.
- Introduced ADP data processing system for payroll, accounts payable and accounts receivable, which reduced time interval between shipment and receipt of payment.

Senior Financial Analyst   **June 1981–June 1985**
- Created credit appraisal system for determining financial risk which was established by regional controller.
- Established a control system to guarantee efficient use of internal operations resulting in annual savings of $7,000.
- Designed computer software to identify profit and loss of existing business.

Staff Analyst   **October 1977–May 1981**
- Implemented computerization of routine management reports which increased unit productivity by over 150%.
- Regulated regional station operations budgets by administering computerized reporting system to locate deviations and trends.
- Appraised effectiveness of sales forecasting techniques.

Controller Trainee   **March 1975–September 1977**
- Projected short-term budget forecast for $4 million computer upgrade which realized savings of $900,000 annually in operating time.
- Evaluated control and monitoring procedures for new maintenance centers.

June 1973–February 1975
Mobil Pipeline Corporation, *Eugene, Oregon*

Pipeliner
- Directed 8-10 contracted hourly employees and was responsible for coordinating, organizing, controlling and supervising a six-month pipeline maintenance project. Surpassed management objective.

EDUCATION
Indiana University, Bloomington, Indiana
Master of Business Administration, 1984
Corporate Finance–Quantitative Analysis

Indiana University, Bloomington, Indiana
Bachelor of Science, 1973
Operations Management

October 13, 1992

Mr. Thomas Hill
Executive Vice President, Marketing and Sales
International Business Machines Corporation
Armonk, NY 10504

Dear Mr. Hill:

I am writing as a result of an article that appeared in the *New York Times* on Sunday, October 11.

According to the report, recent developments in computer robotics threaten IBM's leadership in a field it virtually founded. Besides competitive threats, recent restructuring has apparently diminished IBM's ability to capitalize on a field which may experience explosive growth in the next 10 years.

Review of my resume will show the kinds of skills and accomplishments which would make me a very valuable member of IBM's team in this field. I believe much can be done with a small team of dedicated professionals to maintain a position of leadership in the industry.

I'll be in New York October 19-21 and would appreciate the opportunity to discuss my ideas with you. I'll contact your office to discuss an appointment time. Enclosed is my resume and a copy of the *Times* article. Thank you, in advance, for your consideration.

Sincerely,

Robert Mitchell

Robert Mitchell

Enclosures (2)

Robert S. Mitchell

9252 Timber Road
Indianapolis, Indiana 46240
(317) 634-5052

HIGHLIGHTS OF QUALIFICATIONS

- 10 years executive level experience in business development and management.
- Managed personnel staff of 50 and budget of over $600,000.
- Quick problem solver while dealing with new concepts, systems and procedures.
- Positive motivator, combining creativity with strong verbal, written and presentation skills.
- Decisive and self-starting in implementation.

EMPLOYMENT HISTORY

1/87–Present *Partner International Corporation (PIC), Indianapolis, Indiana*
Vice President, Marketing & Sales

Report to the President of PIC which develops and markets computer software and integrates peripheral devices for multiple vertical markets. Manage over 50 sales, technical and administrative employees generating over $5 million in annual revenue from product sales and consulting. Oversee the sales, marketing, field operations and customer support of ten North American sales regions. Developed a strategic business plan that reversed pretax profits from minus 10% of sales to plus 10% of sales in first year. Restructured domestic sales force coverage that tripled market coverage.

1/81–12/86 *STC Services, Inc., Indianapolis, Indiana*
President & Chief Operating Officer
Vice President, Marketing & Sales

Repositioned company from being in the "timesharing business" to being a "software provider and VAR" for four vendors. Developed a sales force and grew revenue to the $3 million range. Implemented marketing plans for multiple vertical markets. Achieved 18% pretax profits first year as President after company lost money in 1980.

2/77–12/80 *Scientific Comps Corporation (SCC), Indianapolis, Indiana*
Branch Manager

Managed 25 employees who designed, developed, installed and supported software applications installed on SCC's IBM mainframes. Rebuilt branch and grew revenue by 52% first year. Branch was third in U.S. in new account production. Named Branch Manager of the Year. Achieved two out of two 100% Clubs.

7/72–1/77 *MBI Corporation, Indianapolis, Indiana*
Account Representative, 6/74–1/77; **Marketing Representative,** 9/73–5/74;
Sales Representative, 11/72–8/73; **Trainee,** 7/72–10/72

Joined MBI as a Sales Trainee and progressed through the ranks above while achieving all potential 100% Clubs.
Recognition: 100% Club, 1973–1976; Regional Sales Leader, 1976; Indianapolis Sales Leader, 1974

EDUCATION

Indiana University-Purdue University, Indianapolis, Indiana
Master of Business Administration, 1980

Indiana University, Bloomington, Indiana
Bachelor of Science in Business, Major in Management, 1972

PROFESSIONAL AFFILIATIONS AND HONORS

Elected to the Board and the Strategic Planning Committee of the Indiana Computer Industry Council (ICIC).

Served as General Chairman of the 1989 and 1990 Annual Meetings of ICIC.

Received the "Indiana Computer Industry Award for Outstanding Service" given at the 1990 ICIC Annual Meeting.

August 17, 1992

Mr. Chris Harmon
Executive Vice President
Marketing
Colgate-Palmolive Company
300 Park Avenue
New York, NY 10022

Dear Mr. Harmon:

If you are currently in need of a seasoned Marketing executive with a demonstrated record of significant marketing contributions, the enclosed resume should be of interest to you.

After completion of an MBA in Marketing, I have successfully managed marketing teams for over 15 years. Career highlights include:

- Identified new market segments for existing products, resulting in a 17% sales increase for a previously stagnant product line.
- Developed, via proprietary research, a meaningful approach to monitoring consumer attitudes and reporting changes on a timely basis. This system led to revision of products and/or advertising campaigns which maintained our company's leadership position.
- Created and executed a series of product seminars for customers and prospects which directly yielded a sales increase of 4%.

Throughout my career, I have aggressively sought necessary information, logically analyzed this information, and developed the products or programs which fit changing market conditions. I would welcome the opportunity to meet and discuss further how my credentials could best be used by Colgate-Palmolive Company.

Thank you for your consideration. I look forward to hearing from you soon.

Sincerely,

Michael Olson

Michael Olson

Excellent Applicant — Definitely Interview

Michael E. Olson

4748 East 84th Street
New York, New York 10036
(216) 674-0090

SUMMARY OF QUALIFICATIONS

• Outstanding track record of marketing accomplishments including: product development, new market penetration and advertising and sales promotion.
• Widely experienced in profit and loss, training and supervision and public relations.
• Creator of numerous and successful telemarketing, direct mail and trade show exhibit programs.
• Results-oriented executive combining problem-solving analytical skills with a strong creative flair.

CAREER HISTORY

OMNICOM, New York, New York
Director, Market Research, April 1988–Present

Major Clients: Gillette, Polaroid, Du Pont, Avon, Walgreens, General Electric, Pillsbury, Holiday Inn

• Established and directed all facilities of agency's marketing research department. Successfully developed the marketing research function into a profit center.
• Interpreted marketing research and recommendations to improve the quality of client decision making.
• Developed a new approach to reporting and interpreting consumer change for management.

BAUSCH & LOMB, NEW PRODUCTS DIVISION, Rochester, New York
Marketing Manager, May 1983–March 1988

• Conceptualized new product designs in current product which were adopted by management, yielding increased sales of $115,000.
• Introduced product line to new market segments, resulting in multiple purchases and a $300,000 improvement in sales.
• Created and facilitated product seminars for customers and prospects.
• Coordinated and conducted training of sales representatives and managers, leading to a $376,000 increase in sales.

PREMARK INTERNATIONAL, HOUSEHOLD PRODUCTS DIVISION, Deerfield, Illinois
Marketing Research Services Manager, May 1979–April 1983
Marketing Research Brand Manager, July 1975–April 1979

• Planned and conducted all marketing research for new consumer household products from idea conception through test market.
• Initiated new products team approach by successfully collaborating with members of virtually every corporate group while conducting several new product projects at various stages of development.
• Hired and trained a research assistant and set up a research library.

EDUCATION

Columbia University, New York, New York
M.B.A., Marketing, 1990

University of Illinois, Champagne, Illinois
B.B.A., Marketing, 1975

PERSONAL

Free to relocate
Fluent in French

SALLY KLEIN
3812 Crescent Drive
Indianapolis, IN 46250
(317) 297-8400

SUMMARY

- Twelve years experience teaching first and third grades.
- Author of Helping Your Child Learn Responsibility.
- Introduced foreign language curriculum for grades K-6.
- Receiver of five Teacher of the Year Awards given by parents and peers.

EDUCATION

Ball State University, Muncie, Indiana
Bachelor of Arts, Elementary Education, 1980
Indiana Certification, Elementary 1-6

TEACHING EXPERIENCE

First Grade Teacher   *Fall 1987 - Present*
Crestview Elementary School   *Indianapolis, IN*

Plan lessons and instruct students in science, reading, spelling, mathematics and French. Identify and provide assistance to children needing special attention with above or below average skills. Teach children to respect each other as well as their elders. Nurture self-esteem and self-confidence.

Third Grade Teacher   *Fall 1980 - Spring 1987*
Crestview Elementary School   *Indianapolis, IN*

Provided a classroom of structure and freedom to balance learning new concepts with enjoying classroom participation. Placed major emphasis on the total growth and needs of the child including intellectual, social, creative, emotional and physical behavior.

First Grade Student Teacher   *Spring 1980*
Wellington Elementary School   *South Bend, IN*

Demonstrated the ability to motivate the first grade child while teaching all classroom subjects. Created a weekly lunch time lesson that used different science experiments in which the students participated.

One hundred years from now it will not matter what my bank account was, the sort of house I lived in, or the kind of car I drove but the world may be different because I was important in the life of a child.

—Anonymous

Sally Klein
3812 Crescent Drive
Indianapolis, Indiana 46250
(317) 297-8400

SUMMARY

- Twelve years experience teaching first and third grades.
- Author of **Helping Your Child Learn Responsibility.**
- Introduced foreign language curriculum for grades K-6.
- Receiver of five Teacher of the Year Awards given by parents and peers.

EDUCATION

Ball State University, Muncie, Indiana
Bachelor of Arts, Elementary Education, 1980
Indiana Certification, Elementary 1-6

TEACHING EXPERIENCE

First Grade Teacher   **Fall 1987 - Present**
Crestview Elementary School   Indianapolis, Indiana

Plan lessons and instruct students in science, reading, spelling, mathematics and French. Identify and provide assistance to children needing special attention with above or below average skills. Teach children to respect each other as well as their elders. Nurture self-esteem and self-confidence.

Third Grade Teacher   **Fall 1980 - Spring 1987**
Crestview Elementary School   Indianapolis, Indiana

Provided a classroom of structure and freedom to balance learning new concepts with enjoying classroom participation. Placed major emphasis on the total growth and needs of the child including intellectual, social, creative, emotional and physical behavior.

First Grade Student Teacher   **Spring 1980**
Wellington Elementary School   South Bend, Indiana

Demonstrated the ability to motivate the first grade child while teaching all classroom subjects. Created a weekly lunch time lesson that used different science experiments in which the students participated.

Susan L. Miller

7450 North College Avenue
Indianapolis, Indiana 46260
(317) 255-1870

Qualifications

- Conductor of more than 100 seminars on communications and marketing topics
- Effective problem solver using excellent written and verbal communication skills
- 10 years experience as a marketing and public relations manager
- Proficient with computers including word processing, database, spreadsheet, desktop publishing and graphics software
- Co-author, editor and designer of *Layout and Editing Techniques for Beginners*

Experience

6/78–Present Owner and Communications Consultant
Graphics Publications, Indianapolis, Indiana

Write, publish and market publications on the subject of communicating through print medium. Advise organizations about establishing and conducting internal and external communications programs as well as dealing with problems related to those programs. Create workshops and seminars presented to professional communicators.

2/88–3/91 Corporate Communications Director
Ellis, Russell & Associates, Inc., Indianapolis, Indiana

Provided communications, editing, desktop publishing, marketing and printing support to corporate headquarters and 12 regional offices of the United States' largest insurance brokerage firm. Published quarterly newsletter mailed to more than 3,000 clients and potential clients. Managed and maintained newsletter mailing list database. Produced status reports for clients; monthly and quarterly sales and production reports and charts; marketing and training aids; brochures; booklets; and manuals.

2/85–1/88 Marketing Manager
American Financial Services, Indianapolis, Indiana

Conducted market research, developed marketing strategies and set up effective working relationships with a major local bank and a data services company. Recruited and trained sales staff. Designed and produced marketing collateral materials and other sales aids. Produced company training videotapes.

11/80–1/85 Public Relations Director
Indianapolis Developmental Center, Indianapolis, Indiana

Developed and administered all internal and external communications programs for Indiana's largest facility serving the mentally and physically handicapped. Directed community education, media relations, printing and audio-visual operations. Evaluated and analyzed programs and resources available in four departments while providing operational guidance and supervision to staff. Edited press releases, annual reports, personnel recruiting materials.

Education

DePauw University, Greencastle, Indiana
Bachelor of Arts in Communications, 1978

"It is not enough to make progress; we must make it in the right direction." —Anonymous

Susan L. Miller

7450 North College Avenue
Indianapolis, Indiana 46260
(317) 255-1870

Qualifications

- Conductor of more than 100 seminars on communications and marketing topics
- Effective problem solver using excellent written and verbal communication skills
- 10 years experience as a marketing and public relations manager
- Proficient with computers including word processing, database, spreadsheet, desktop publishing and graphics software
- Co-author, editor and designer of *Layout and Editing Techniques for Beginners*

Experience

6/78–PRESENT OWNER AND COMMUNICATIONS CONSULTANT
Graphics Publications, Indianapolis, Indiana

Write, publish and market publications on the subject of communicating through print medium. Advise organizations about establishing and conducting internal and external communications programs as well as dealing with problems related to those programs. Create workshops and seminars presented to professional communicators.

2/88–3/91 CORPORATE COMMUNICATIONS DIRECTOR
Ellis, Russell & Associates, Inc., Indianapolis, Indiana

Provided communications, editing, desktop publishing, marketing and printing support to corporate headquarters and 12 regional offices of the United States' largest brokerage firm. Published quarterly newsletter mailed to more than 3,000 clients and potential clients. Managed and maintained newsletter mailing list database. Produced status reports for clients; monthly and quarterly sales and production reports and charts; marketing and training aids; brochures; booklets; and manuals.

2/85–1/88 MARKETING MANAGER
American Financial Services, Indianapolis, Indiana

Conducted market research, developed marketing strategies and set up effective working relationships with a major local bank and a data services company. Recruited and trained sales staff. Designed and produced marketing collateral materials and other sales aids. Produced company training videotapes.

11/80–1/85 PUBLIC RELATIONS DIRECTOR
Indianapolis Developmental Center, Indianapolis, Indiana

Developed and administered all internal and external communications programs for Indiana's largest facility serving the mentally and physically handicapped. Directed community education, media relations, printing and audio-visual operations. Evaluated and analyzed programs and resources available in four departments while providing operational guidance and supervision to staff. Edited press releases, annual reports, personnel recruiting materials.

Education

DePauw University, Greencastle, Indiana
Bachelor of Arts in Communications, 1978

Andrew Freeman

□

7181 North Cooper Street
Indianapolis, Indiana 46220
(317) 844-8909

This resume is a
4-page format.
It is also
distinguished
by an unusual
size—6.5x11
after folding.
The "edge" of
the paper is
indicated by
this line.

ANDREW FREEMAN
7181 North Cooper Street
Indianapolis, Indiana 46220
(317) 844-8909

SUMMARY OF QUALIFICATIONS
- Successfully managed budgets in excess of $5 million.
- Experienced in developing short- and long-term financial business planning.
- Effective problem solver using excellent written and verbal communication skills.
- Demonstrated expertise in operations consolidation and divestiture.

This resume is a 4-page format. It is also distinguished by an unusual size—6.5x11 after folding. The "edge" of the paper is indicated by this line.

■ **EMPLOYMENT HISTORY**

March 1975–Present
Shell Oil Corporation, *Indianapolis, Indiana*

Supervisor, Financial Analyst   **July 1985–Present**
- Manage, train and develop seven MBA analysts responsible for systems development and financial planning to optimize return on investment, evaluate long range resource requirements and organize management sciences activities.
- Consolidated all economic planning within controller's portfolio by implementing departmental reorganization.
- Initiated proposal to optimize manufacturing facility which increased productivity 175%.
- Introduced ADP data processing system for payroll, accounts payable and accounts receivable, which reduced time interval between shipment and receipt of payment.

Senior Financial Analyst   **June 1981–June 1985**
- Created credit appraisal system for determining financial risk which was established by regional controller.
- Established a control system to guarantee efficient use of internal operations resulting in annual savings of $7,000.
- Designed computer software to identify profit and loss of existing business.

Staff Analyst   **October 1977–May 1981**
- Implemented computerization of routine management reports which increased unit productivity by over 150%.
- Regulated regional station operations budgets by administering computerized reporting system to locate deviations and trends.
- Appraised effectiveness of sales forecasting techniques.

Controller Trainee   **March 1975–September 1977**
- Projected short-term budget forecast for $4 million computer upgrade which realized savings of $900,000 annually in operating time.
- Evaluated control and monitoring procedures for new maintenance centers.

June 1973–February 1975
Mobil Pipeline Corporation, *Eugene, Oregon*

Pipeliner
- Directed 8-10 contracted hourly employees and was responsible for coordinating, organizing, controlling and supervising a six-month pipeline maintenance project. Surpassed management objective.

 The "edge" of the paper is indicated by this line.

EDUCATION
Indiana University, Bloomington, Indiana
Master of Business Administration, 1984
Corporate Finance–Quantitative Analysis

Indiana University, Bloomington, Indiana
Bachelor of Science, 1973
Operations Management

HELEN M. YOUNG
3003 North Lincoln Avenue
Indianapolis, Indiana 46208
(317) 279-7900

AREAS OF ACHIEVEMENT

PUBLIC RELATIONS
- Coordinated and established an Information/Media Center in the Republic of the Philippines. Initiated and wrote press releases, answered queries and directed photo opportunities.
- Provided positive publicity in Japan for the American community on nationwide and local Japanese television.
- Established ongoing working rapport with the American Embassy and the International Press Center in Japan and the Republic of the Philippines.

COMMUNICATIONS
- Initiated on-camera media training for CEO's.
- Spoke for the Navy in Washington, D.C. concerning a wide variety of issues with leading national and international media representatives. Participated on an education steering committee related to an HIV/AIDS education film to be distributed Navy-wide.
- Developed and executed comprehensive training programs from concept to delivery. Instructed 2,000 U.S. and foreign public relations students annually in the area of public relations, media relations, internal information, electronic news gathering, editing and planning.
- Arranged, organized and conducted tours, sporting events and social functions, for the internal audience, general public and media representatives in 12 countries with participation ranging from 500 to 12,000.

MANAGEMENT
- Supervised the daily performance of 4 separate public relations offices which worked to solve public relations problems in the U.S. and overseas.
- Prepared budgets for five different offices.
- Recruited and trained over 55 employees.
- Coordinated purchasing for offices of 75 staff.

WORK EXPERIENCE

1988-Present ASSISTANT PROFESSOR, Defense Information School, Fort Benjamin Harris, Indianapolis, Indiana

1984-1987 PUBLIC AFFAIRS OFFICER, Navy Bureau of Medicine & Surgery, Washington, D.C.

1982-1983 DIRECTOR—SPEAKERS BUREAU, Bureau of Navy Information, The Pentagon, Washington, D.C.

1980-1981 MEDIA OFFICER, Bureau of Navy Information, The Pentagon, Washington, D.C.

1975-1979 PUBLIC AFFAIRS OFFICER, Naval Security Group Activity, Misawa, Japan

EDUCATION

Butler University, Indianapolis, Indiana
Master of Arts, Communication, 1975

University of Illinois, Champaign, Illinois
Bachelor of Science, Public Relations and Japanese, 1973

CERTIFICATES OF COMPLETION

Defense Information School, Indianapolis, Indiana
- Public Affairs Officer Course, 1975
- Electronic News Gathering & Editing Techniques, 1975
- Television Production, 1975

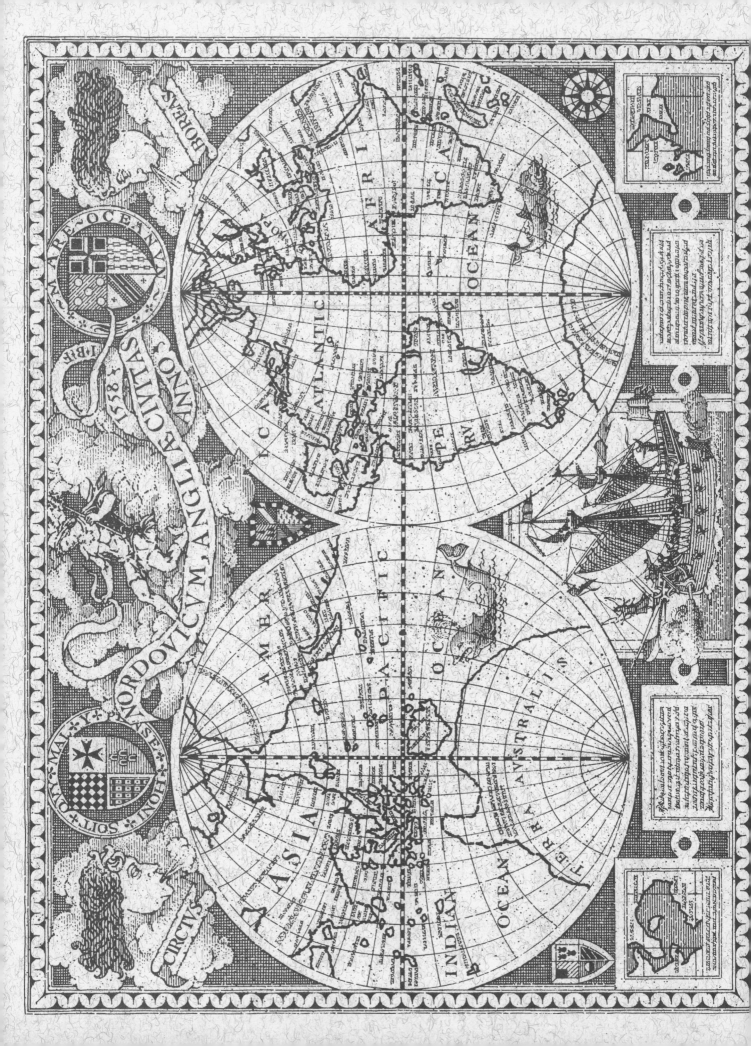

Helen M. Young

3003 North Lincoln Avenue
Indianapolis, Indiana 46208
(317) 279-7900

AREAS OF ACHIEVEMENT

PUBLIC RELATIONS
- Coordinated and established an Information/Media Center in the Republic of the Philippines. Initiated and wrote press releases, answered queries and directed photo opportunities.
- Provided positive publicity in Japan for the American community on nationwide and local Japanese television.
- Established ongoing working rapport with the American Embassy and the International Press Center in Japan and the Republic of the Philippines.

COMMUNICATIONS
- Initiated on-camera media training for CEO's.
- Spoke for the Navy in Washington, D.C. concerning a wide variety of issues with leading national and international media representatives. Participated on an education steering committee related to an HIV/AIDS education film to be distributed Navy-wide.
- Developed and executed comprehensive training programs from concept to delivery. Instructed 2,000 U.S. and foreign public relations students annually in the area of public relations, media relations, internal information, electronic news gathering, editing and planning.
- Arranged, organized and conducted tours, sporting events and social functions, for the internal audience, general public and media representatives in 12 countries with participation ranging from 500 to 12,000.

MANAGEMENT
- Supervised the daily performance of 4 separate public relations offices which worked to solve public relations problems in the U.S. and overseas.
- Prepared budgets for five different offices.
- Recruited and trained over 55 employees.
- Coordinated purchasing for offices of 75 staff.

WORK EXPERIENCE

1988-Present *ASSISTANT PROFESSOR,* Defense Information School, Fort Benjamin Harris, Indianapolis, IN

1984-1987 *PUBLIC AFFAIRS OFFICER,* Navy Bureau of Medicine & Surgery, Washington, D.C.

1982-1983 *DIRECTOR—SPEAKERS BUREAU,* Bureau of Navy Information, The Pentagon, Washington, D.C.

1980-1981 *MEDIA OFFICER,* Bureau of Navy Information, The Pentagon, Washington, D.C.

1975-1979 *PUBLIC AFFAIRS OFFICER,* Naval Security Group Activity, Misawa, Japan

EDUCATION

Butler University, Indianapolis, Indiana
Master of Arts, Communication, 1975

University of Illinois, Champaign, Illinois
Bachelor of Science, Public Relations and Japanese, 1973

CERTIFICATES OF COMPLETION

Defense Information School, Indianapolis, Indiana
- Public Affairs Officer Course, 1975
- Electronic News Gathering & Editing Techniques, 1975
- Television Production, 1975

Robert S. Mitchell

9252 Timber Road
Indianapolis, Indiana 46240
(317) 634-5052

HIGHLIGHTS OF QUALIFICATIONS

- 10 years executive level experience in business development and management.
- Managed personnel staff of 50 and budget of over $600,000.
- Quick problem solver while dealing with new concepts, systems and procedures.
- Positive motivator, combining creativity with strong verbal, written and presentation skills.
- Decisive and self-starting in implementation.

EMPLOYMENT HISTORY

1/87–Present

Partner International Corporation (PIC), Indianapolis, Indiana
Vice President, Marketing & Sales

Report to the President of PIC which develops and markets computer software and integrates peripheral devices for multiple vertical markets. Manage over 50 sales, technical and administrative employees generating over $5 million in annual revenue from product sales and consulting. Oversee the sales, marketing, field operations and customer support of ten North American sales regions. Developed a strategic business plan that reversed pretax profits from minus 10% of sales to plus 10% of sales in first year. Restructured domestic sales force coverage that tripled market coverage.

1/81–12/86

STC Services, Inc., Indianapolis, Indiana
President & Chief Operating Officer
Vice President, Marketing & Sales

Repositioned company from being in the "timesharing business" to being a "software provider and VAR" for four vendors. Developed a sales force and grew revenue to the $3 million range. Implemented marketing plans for multiple vertical markets. Achieved 18% pretax profits first year as President after company lost money in 1980.

2/77–12/80

Scientific Comps Corporation (SCC), Indianapolis, Indiana
Branch Manager

Managed 25 employees who designed, developed, installed and supported software applications installed on SCC's IBM mainframes. Rebuilt branch and grew revenue by 52% first year. Branch was third in U.S. in new account production. Named Branch Manager of the Year. Achieved two out of two 100% Clubs.

7/72–1/77

MBI Corporation, Indianapolis, Indiana
Account Representative, 6/74–1/77; **Marketing Representative**, 9/73–5/74;
Sales Representative, 11/72–8/73; **Trainee**, 7/72–10/72

Joined MBI as a Sales Trainee and progressed through the ranks above while achieving all potential 100% Clubs.
Recognition: 100% Club, 1973–1976; Regional Sales Leader, 1976; Indianapolis Sales Leader, 1974

EDUCATION

Indiana University-Purdue University, Indianapolis, Indiana
Master of Business Administration, 1980

Indiana University, Bloomington, Indiana
Bachelor of Science in Business, Major in Management, 1972

PROFESSIONAL AFFILIATIONS AND HONORS

Elected to the Board and the Strategic Planning Committee of the Indiana Computer Industry Council (ICIC).

Served as General Chairman of the 1989 and 1990 Annual Meetings of ICIC.

Received the "Indiana Computer Industry Award for Outstanding Service" given at the 1990 ICIC Annual Meeting.

SUSAN L. MILLER

7450 North College Avenue
Indianapolis, Indiana 46260
(317) 255-1870

HIGHLIGHTS OF QUALIFICATIONS

- Conductor of more than 100 seminars on communications and marketing topics
- Effective problem solver using excellent written and verbal communication skills
- 10 years experience as a marketing and public relations manager
- Proficient with computers including word processing, database, spreadsheet, desktop publishing and graphics software
- Co-author, editor and designer of *Layout and Editing Techniques for Beginners*

PROFESSIONAL EXPERIENCE

6/78–Present Owner and Communications Consultant
Graphics Publications, Indianapolis, Indiana

Write, publish and market publications on the subject of communicating through print medium. Advise organizations about establishing and conducting internal and external communications programs as well as dealing with problems related to those programs. Create workshops and seminars presented to professional communicators.

2/88–3/91 Corporate Communications Director
Ellis, Russell & Associates, Inc., Indianapolis, Indiana

Provided communications, editing, desktop publishing, marketing and printing support to corporate headquarters and 12 regional offices of the United States' largest insurance brokerage firm. Published quarterly newsletter mailed to more than 3,000 clients and potential clients. Managed and maintained newsletter mailing list database. Produced status reports for clients; monthly and quarterly sales and production reports and charts; marketing and training aids; brochures; booklets; and manuals.

2/85–1/88 Marketing Manager
American Financial Services, Indianapolis, Indiana

Conducted market research, developed marketing strategies and set up effective working relationships with a major local bank and a data services company. Recruited and trained sales staff. Designed and produced marketing collateral materials and other sales aids. Produced company training videotapes.

11/80–1/85 Public Relations Director
Indianapolis Developmental Center, Indianapolis, Indiana

Developed and administered all internal and external communications programs for Indiana's largest facility serving the mentally and physically handicapped. Directed community education, media relations, printing and audio-visual operations. Evaluated and analyzed programs and resources available in four departments while providing operational guidance and supervision to staff. Edited press releases, annual reports, personnel recruiting materials.

EDUCATION

DePauw University, Greencastle, Indiana
Bachelor of Arts in Communications, 1978

Laura Dobbs
8565 North Oak Street, Indianapolis, Indiana 46260, (317) 844-6500

SUMMARY
- Fifteen years accounting experience with a strong background in auditing, business and individual taxes and cost control programs.
- Excellent management skills. Consistently obtain high productivity from employees.
- Efficient in implementing computerized accounting systems and designing more effective manual systems.
- Rapidly recognize and analyze company problems and solutions.

EDUCATION
Certified Public Accountant, 1980
Indiana State Certification

Indiana University, Bloomington, Indiana
Bachelor of Science, 1977
> *Major:* Accounting
> *Minor:* Business Administration

PROFESSIONAL EXPERIENCE
Cost Accounting
Implemented cost accounting systems.
- Developed a major cost control program that cut overhead 15%.
- Reduced costs for small businesses and large corporations.
- Established complete integrated accounting package for entire corporations.

Accounting and Budgeting
Converted manual accounting systems to efficient computerized office systems for several companies throughout the Indianapolis area.
- Designed, installed and implemented effective budgeting systems under cash and accrual accounting methods.
- Established accounting procedures which sigigicantly reduced errors and duplication of effort by 55%.
- Successfully tracked and reduced costs for multi-million dollar contracts.

Auditing
Performed audits and developed financial statements for a wide variety of clients.
Audited multi-million dollar subcontractors accounting records and facilities for government contracts.
Trained employees to comply with new state accounting regulations and identified accounting and operational irregularities.

Management and Administration
Reported directly to the President. Responsible for Accounting, Data Processing, Procurement Analysis and Review Departments' reports.
- Hired, trained and managed 5-40 employees.
- Set up and conducted monthly motivational staff meetings.
Extensively involved in customer relations, establishing credit ratings, approving credit, reviewing and approving customer claims and making collections.

"A PENNY
SAVED IS A
PENNY
THAT GOES
TO THE
BOTTOM
LINE."

EMPLOYMENT HISTORY

1988–Present	*Controller,* Indiana Bell, Indianapolis, Indiana
1981–1988	*Controller,* Cummins Engine, Columbus, Indiana
1977–1981	*Staff Accountant*, Arthur Andersen & Co., Indianapolis, Indiana

Michael E. Olson

Career History

Bausch & Lomb, New Products Division, *New York, New York*

Marketing Manager
May 1988-Present

Conceptualized new product designs in current product which were adopted by management, yielding increased sales of $115,000.

Introduced product line to new market segments, resulting in multiple purchases and a $300,000 improvement in sales.

Created and facilitated product seminars for customers and prospects.

Coordinated and conducted training of sales representatives and managers, leading to a $376,000 increase in sales.

Premark International, Household Products Division, *Deerfield, Illinois*

Marketing Research Services Manager
May 1984-April 1988

Marketing Research Brand Manager
July 1980-April 1984

Planned and conducted all marketing research for new consumer household products from idea conception through test market.

Initiated new products team approach by successfully collaborating with members of virtually every corporate group while conducting several new product projects at various stages of development.

Hired and trained a research assistant and set up a research library.

Summary

Outstanding track record of marketing accomplishments including: product development, new market penetration and advertising and sales promotion.

Widely experienced in profit and loss, training and supervision, and public relations.

Creator of numerous and successful telemarketing, direct mail and trade show exhibit programs.

Results-oriented executive combining problem-solving analytical skills with a strong creative flair.

Education

Columbia University
New York, New York
M.B.A., Marketing, 1990

University of Illinois
Champagne, Illinois
B.B.A., Marketing, 1975

Address

4748 East 84th Street
New York, New York 10036

(216) 674-0090

CHRISTOPHER L. WHITE

3130 West Jordan Drive
Indianapolis, Indiana 46220
(317) 844-5052

HIGHLIGHTS OF QUALIFICATIONS

- 16 years successful experience in office products and computer hardware and software systems sales
- Positive motivator, combining creativity with strong verbal and written skills
- Receiver of numerous recognition awards for outstanding achievement as a sales manager and account representative

EDUCATION

Butler University, Indianapolis, Indiana
Bachelor of Arts in English, 1979

EMPLOYMENT HISTORY

8/82–Present
COMPUTER SOLUTIONS, INC.
Indianapolis, Indiana

Manager, Strategic Accounts & Specialized Markets, 7/90–Present
Responsible for profitability and marketing efforts within the major account marketplace of Indianapolis. Developed plans to penetrate specific niche vertical markets with the objective of maintaining higher margins through an applications/solutions sale instead of a pure hardware/software focus. Exceeded margins of 33 points and secured 15 non-profit association headquarters in less than 3 years.

General Manager, 1/87–7/90
Responsible for a systems integration sales and service business with focus on LAN/WAN technologies, database applications, consulting and information management. Implemented sales relationships with major accounts in the target markets of 3 states. Managed a staff of 20 sales, technical and administrative employees generating over $5,000,000 in annual revenue from product sales, consulting and modeling through design, implementation and testing.

Sales Manager, 8/82–1/87
Set up new office for Computer Solutions in Indiana. Recruited and interviewed potential employees. Marketed full line of office automation products to both major accounts and new customers in Central Indiana. Promoted to General Manager based on success as Sales Manager.

Recognition:
President's Award–1983
Top Branch Office–1984, 1986, 1987, 1988
Corporate Revenue Sales Leader–1984, 1985, 1987

6/79–7/82
PHI BETA ALPHA GENERAL FRATERNITY
Indianapolis, Indiana

Director of Expansion, 7/80–7/82
Traveled to colleges within the region to discuss the acquisition, programming and installation of new college chapters. Served as liaison to college administrators and spoke to prospective chapters on financial management and group dynamics.

Chapter Consultant, 6/79–7/80
Visited 70 college and university campuses throughout the U.S. and Canada to evaluate and counsel undergraduate officers and alumni on improving chapter operations.

COLLEGE HONORS

Dean's List, Gold Key Honorary, Who's Who in American Colleges & Universities
Fraternity Chapter President, Outstanding Senior, President's Award

Andrew Freeman
7181 North Cooper Street
Indianapolis, Indiana 46220
(317) 844-8909

SUMMARY OF QUALIFICATIONS
- Successfully managed budgets in excess of $5 million.
- Experienced in developing short- and long-term financial business planning.
- Effective problem solver using excellent written and verbal communication skills.
- Demonstrated expertise in operations consolidation and divestiture.

EMPLOYMENT HISTORY

March 1975–Present
Shell Oil Corporation, *Indianapolis, Indiana*

Supervisor, Financial Analyst   **July 1985–Present**
- Manage, train and develop seven MBA analysts responsible for systems development and financial planning to optimize return on investment, evaluate long range resource requirements and organize management sciences activities.
- Consolidated all economic planning within controller's portfolio by implementing departmental reorganization.
- Initiated proposal to optimize manufacturing facility which increased productivity 175%.
- Introduced ADP data processing system for payroll, accounts payable and accounts receivable, which reduced time interval between shipment and receipt of payment.

Senior Financial Analyst   **June 1981–June 1985**
- Created credit appraisal system for determining financial risk which was established by regional controller.
- Established a control system to guarantee efficient use of internal operations resulting in annual savings of $7,000.
- Designed computer software to identify profit and loss of existing business.

Staff Analyst   **October 1977–May 1981**
- Implemented computerization of routine management reports which increased unit productivity by over 150%.
- Regulated regional station operations budgets by administering computerized reporting system to locate deviations and trends.
- Appraised effectiveness of sales forecasting techniques.

Controller Trainee   **March 1975–September 1977**
- Projected short-term budget forecast for $4 million computer upgrade which realized savings of $900,000 annually in operating time.
- Evaluated control and monitoring procedures for new maintenance centers.

June 1973–February 1975
Mobil Pipeline Corporation, *Eugene, Oregon*

Pipeliner
- Directed 8-10 contracted hourly employees and was responsible for coordinating, organizing, controlling and supervising a six-month pipeline maintenance project. Surpassed management objective.

EDUCATION
Indiana University, Bloomington, Indiana
Master of Business Administration, 1984
Corporate Finance–Quantitative Analysis

Indiana University, Bloomington, Indiana
Bachelor of Science, 1973
Operations Management

Laura Dobbs

8565 North Oak Street, Indianapolis, Indiana 46260
(317) 844-6500

SUMMARY

- Fifteen years accounting experience with a strong background in auditing, business and individual taxes and cost control programs.
- Excellent management skills. Consistently obtain high productivity from employees.
- Efficient in implementing computerized accounting systems and designing more effective manual systems.
- Rapidly recognize and analyze company problems and solutions.

EDUCATION

Certified Public Accountant, 1980
Indiana State Certification

Indiana University, Bloomington, Indiana
Bachelor of Science, 1977
   Major: Accounting
   Minor: Business Administration

PROFESSIONAL EXPERIENCE

Cost Accounting
Implemented cost accounting systems.
- Developed a major cost control program that cut overhead 15%.
- Reduced costs for small businesses and large corporations.
- Established complete integrated accounting package for entire corporations.

Accounting and Budgeting
Converted manual accounting systems to efficient computerized office systems for several companies throughout the Indianapolis area.
- Designed, installed and implemented effective budgeting systems under cash and accrual accounting methods.
- Established accounting procedures which signigicantly reduced errors and duplication of effort by 55%.
- Successfully tracked and reduced costs for multi-million dollar contracts.

Auditing
Performed audits and developed financial statements for a wide variety of clients.
Audited multi-million dollar subcontractors accounting records and facilities for government contracts.
Trained employees to comply with new state accounting regulations and identified accounting and operational irregularities.

Management and Administration
Reported directly to the President. Responsible for Accounting, Data Processing, Procurement Analysis and Review Departments' reports.
- Hired, trained and managed 5-40 employees.
- Set up and conducted monthly motivational staff meetings.
Extensively involved in customer relations, establishing credit ratings, approving credit, reviewing and approving customer claims and making collections.

EMPLOYMENT HISTORY

1988–Present	**Controller,** Indiana Bell, Indianapolis, Indiana
1981–1988	**Controller,** Cummins Engine, Columbus, Indiana
1977–1981	**Staff Accountant,** Arthur Andersen & Co., Indianapolis, Indiana

Helen M. Young

3003 North Lincoln Avenue
Indianapolis, Indiana 46208
(317) 279-7900

AREAS OF ACHIEVEMENT

PUBLIC RELATIONS
- Coordinated and established an Information/Media Center in the Republic of the Philippines. Initiated and wrote press releases, answered queries and directed photo opportunities.
- Provided positive publicity in Japan for the American community on nationwide and local Japanese television.
- Established ongoing working rapport with the American Embassy and the International Press Center in Japan and the Republic of the Philippines.

COMMUNICATIONS
- Initiated on-camera media training for CEO's.
- Spoke for the Navy in Washington, D.C. concerning a wide variety of issues with leading national and international media representatives. Participated on an education steering committee related to an HIV/AIDS education film to be distributed Navy-wide.
- Developed and executed comprehensive training programs from concept to delivery. Instructed 2,000 U.S. and foreign public relations students annually in the area of public relations, media relations, internal information, electronic news gathering, editing and planning.
- Arranged, organized and conducted tours, sporting events and social functions, for the internal audience, general public and media representatives in 12 countries with participation ranging from 500 to 12,000.

MANAGEMENT
- Supervised the daily performance of 4 separate public relations offices which worked to solve public relations problems in the U.S. and overseas.
- Prepared budgets for five different offices.
- Recruited and trained over 55 employees.
- Coordinated purchasing for offices of 75 staff.

WORK EXPERIENCE

1988-Present   **Assistant Professor,** Defense Information School, Fort Benjamin Harris, Indianapolis, Indiana

1984-1987   **Public Affairs Officer,** Navy Bureau of Medicine & Surgery, Washington, D.C.

1982-1983   **Director—Speakers Bureau,** Bureau of Navy Information, The Pentagon, Washington, D.C.

1980-1981   **Media Officer,** Bureau of Navy Information, The Pentagon, Washington, D.C.

1975-1979   **Public Affairs Officer,** Naval Security Group Activity, Misawa, Japan

EDUCATION

Butler University, Indianapolis, Indiana
Master of Arts, Communication, 1975

University of Illinois, Champaign, Illinois
Bachelor of Science, Public Relations and Japanese, 1973

CERTIFICATES OF COMPLETION

Defense Information School, Indianapolis, Indiana
- Public Affairs Officer Course, 1975
- Electronic News Gathering & Editing Techniques, 1975
- Television Production, 1975

Andrew Freeman

7181 North Cooper Street
Indianapolis, Indiana 46220
(317) 844-8909

SUMMARY OF QUALIFICATIONS
- Successfully managed budgets in excess of $5 million.
- Experienced in developing short- and long-term financial business planning.
- Effective problem solver using excellent written and verbal communication skills.
- Demonstrated expertise in operations consolidation and divestiture.

EMPLOYMENT HISTORY

March 1975–Present
Shell Oil Corporation, *Indianapolis, Indiana*

Supervisor, Financial Analyst   **July 1985–Present**
- Manage, train and develop seven MBA analysts responsible for systems development and financial planning to optimize return on investment, evaluate long range resource requirements and organize management sciences activities.
- Consolidated all economic planning within controller's portfolio by implementing departmental reorganization.
- Initiated proposal to optimize manufacturing facility which increased productivity 175%.
- Introduced ADP data processing system for payroll, accounts payable and accounts receivable, which reduced time interval between shipment and receipt of payment.

Senior Financial Analyst   **June 1981–June 1985**
- Created credit appraisal system for determining financial risk which was established by regional controller.
- Established a control system to guarantee efficient use of internal operations resulting in annual savings of $7,000.
- Designed computer software to identify profit and loss of existing business.

Staff Analyst   **October 1977–May 1981**
- Implemented computerization of routine management reports which increased unit productivity by over 150%.
- Regulated regional station operations budgets by administering computerized reporting system to locate deviations and trends.
- Appraised effectiveness of sales forecasting techniques.

Controller Trainee   **March 1975–September 1977**
- Projected short-term budget forecast for $4 million computer upgrade which realized savings of $900,000 annually in operating time.
- Evaluated control and monitoring procedures for new maintenance centers.

June 1973–February 1975
Mobil Pipeline Corporation, *Eugene, Oregon*

Pipeliner
- Directed 8-10 contracted hourly employees and was responsible for coordinating, organizing, controlling and supervising a six-month pipeline maintenance project. Surpassed management objective.

EDUCATION
Indiana University, Bloomington, Indiana
Master of Business Administration, 1984
Corporate Finance–Quantitative Analysis

Indiana University, Bloomington, Indiana
Bachelor of Science, 1973
Operations Management

97

Robert S. Mitchell

9252 Timber Road
Indianapolis, Indiana 46240
(317) 634-5052

HIGHLIGHTS OF QUALIFICATIONS

- 10 years executive level experience in business development and management.
- Managed personnel staff of 50 and budget of over $600,000.
- Quick problem solver while dealing with new concepts, systems and procedures.
- Positive motivator, combining creativity with strong verbal, written and presentation skills.
- Decisive and self-starting in implementation.

EMPLOYMENT HISTORY

1/87–Present   *Partner International Corporation (PIC), Indianapolis, Indiana*
Vice President, Marketing & Sales

Report to the President of PIC which develops and markets computer software and integrates peripheral devices for multiple vertical markets. Manage over 50 sales, technical and administrative employees generating over $5 million in annual revenue from product sales and consulting. Oversee the sales, marketing, field operations and customer support of ten North American sales regions. Developed a strategic business plan that reversed pretax profits from minus 10% of sales to plus 10% of sales in first year. Restructured domestic sales force coverage that tripled market coverage.

1/81–12/86   *STC Services, Inc., Indianapolis, Indiana*
President & Chief Operating Officer
Vice President, Marketing & Sales

Repositioned company from being in the "timesharing business" to being a "software provider and VAR" for four vendors. Developed a sales force and grew revenue to the $3 million range. Implemented marketing plans for multiple vertical markets. Achieved 18% pretax profits first year as President after company lost money in 1980.

2/77–12/80   *Scientific Comps Corporation (SCC), Indianapolis, Indiana*
Branch Manager

Managed 25 employees who designed, developed, installed and supported software applications installed on SCC's IBM mainframes. Rebuilt branch and grew revenue by 52% first year. Branch was third in U.S. in new account production. Named Branch Manager of the Year. Achieved two out of two 100% Clubs.

7/72–1/77   *MBI Corporation, Indianapolis, Indiana*
Account Representative, 6/74–1/77; **Marketing Representative**, 9/73–5/74;
Sales Representative, 11/72–8/73; **Trainee**, 7/72–10/72

Joined MBI as a Sales Trainee and progressed through the ranks above while achieving all potential 100% Clubs.
Recognition: 100% Club, 1973–1976; Regional Sales Leader, 1976; Indianapolis Sales Leader, 1974

EDUCATION

Indiana University-Purdue University, Indianapolis, Indiana
Master of Business Administration, 1980

Indiana University, Bloomington, Indiana
Bachelor of Science in Business, Major in Management, 1972

PROFESSIONAL AFFILIATIONS AND HONORS

Elected to the Board and the Strategic Planning Committee of the Indiana Computer Industry Council (ICIC).

Served as General Chairman of the 1989 and 1990 Annual Meetings of ICIC.

Received the "Indiana Computer Industry Award for Outstanding Service" given at the 1990 ICIC Annual Meeting.

Laura Dobbs
8565 North Oak Street, Indianapolis, Indiana 46260, (317) 844-6500

SUMMARY
- Fifteen years accounting experience with a strong background in auditing, business and individual taxes and cost control programs.
- Excellent management skills. Consistently obtain high productivity from employees.
- Efficient in implementing computerized accounting systems and designing more effective manual systems.
- Rapidly recognize and analyze company problems and solutions.

EDUCATION
Certified Public Accountant, 1980
Indiana State Certification

Indiana University, Bloomington, Indiana
Bachelor of Science, 1977
     Major: Accounting
     Minor: Business Administration

PROFESSIONAL EXPERIENCE
Cost Accounting
Implemented cost accounting systems.
- Developed a major cost control program that cut overhead 15%.
- Reduced costs for small businesses and large corporations.
- Established complete integrated accounting package for entire corporations.

Accounting and Budgeting
Converted manual accounting systems to efficient computerized office systems for several companies throughout the Indianapolis area.
- Designed, installed and implemented effective budgeting systems under cash and accrual accounting methods.
- Established accounting procedures which signigicantly reduced errors and duplication of effort by 55%.
- Successfully tracked and reduced costs for multi-million dollar contracts.

Auditing
Performed audits and developed financial statements for a wide variety of clients.
Audited multi-million dollar subcontractors accounting records and facilities for government contracts.
Trained employees to comply with new state accounting regulations and identified accounting and operational irregularities.

Management and Administration
Reported directly to the President. Responsible for Accounting, Data Processing, Procurement Analysis and Review Departments' reports.
- Hired, trained and managed 5-40 employees.
- Set up and conducted monthly motivational staff meetings.
Extensively involved in customer relations, establishing credit ratings, approving credit, reviewing and approving customer claims and making collections.

EMPLOYMENT HISTORY
1988–Present	*Controller,* Indiana Bell, Indianapolis, Indiana
1981–1988	*Controller,* Cummins Engine, Columbus, Indiana
1977–1981	*Staff Accountant,* Arthur Andersen & Co., Indianapolis, Indiana

Michael E. Olson

4748 East 84th Street
New York, New York 10036
(216) 674-0090

SUMMARY OF QUALIFICATIONS

- *Outstanding track record of marketing accomplishments including: product development, new market penetration and advertising and sales promotion.*
- *Widely experienced in profit and loss, training and supervision and public relations.*
- *Creator of numerous and successful telemarketing, direct mail and trade show exhibit programs.*
- *Results-oriented executive combining problem-solving analytical skills with a strong creative flair.*

CAREER HISTORY

OMNICOM, *New York, New York*
Director, Market Research, *April 1988–Present*

Major Clients: *Gillette, Polaroid, Du Pont, Avon, Walgreens, General Electric, Pillsbury, Holiday Inn*

- *Established and directed all facilities of agency's marketing research department. Successfully developed the marketing research function into a profit center, an unprecedented accomplishment for the agency.*
- *Improved the quality of client and agency management decision making and new business presentations through interpretation of marketing research and recommendations. Helped agency attract two new client accounts through presentation of marketing recommendations derived from marketing research.*
- *Developed, via proprietary research, a meaningful approach to reporting and interpreting consumer change for management.*

BAUSCH & LOMB, NEW PRODUCTS DIVISION, *Rochester, New York*
Marketing Manager, *May 1983–March 1988*

- *Conceptualized new product designs in current product which were adopted by management, yielding increased sales of $115,000.*
- *Introduced product line to new market segments, resulting in multiple purchases and a $300,000 improvement in sales.*
- *Created and facilitated first company-run product seminars for customers and prospects. Result was a gain in awareness and a $164,000 sales increase.*
- *Coordinated and conducted training of sales representatives and Regional Sales Managers, leading to a $376,000 increase in sales.*

PREMARK INTERNATIONAL, HOUSEHOLD PRODUCTS DIVISION, *Deerfield, Illinois*
Marketing Research Services Manager, *May 1979–April 1983*
Marketing Research Brand Manager, *July 1975–April 1979*

- *Planned and conducted all marketing research for new consumer household products from idea conception through test market.*
- *Initiated new products team approach by successfully collaborating with members of virtually every corporate group while conducting several new product projects at various stages of development.*
- *Hired and trained a research assistant and set up a research library.*

EDUCATION

Columbia University, *New York, New York*
M.B.A., Marketing, 1990

University of Illinois, *Champagne, Illinois*
B.B.A., Marketing, 1975

PERSONAL

Free to relocate
Fluent in French

Introduced product line to new market segments, resulting in multiple purchases and a $300,000 improvement in sales.

CAROLYN P. LAWSON
545 West 78th Street
Indianapolis, IN 46220

HIGHLIGHTS OF QUALIFICATIONS

Strong ability to present and sell tangible as well as intangible goods through the use of the telephone.
Seven years experience in the field of telemarketing and inside sales.
Think quickly on my feet and am able to maintain a sense of humor under pressure and deadlines.

EDUCATION

Purdue University, West Lafayette, Indiana
Bachelor of Arts in Communication, 1985

PROFESSIONAL ACCOMPLISHMENTS

SPEAKING and PRESENTATION SKILLS

Educated customers on the advantages of advertising while using a clear and pleasing tone of voice.
Proposed strategic Yellow Pages programs over the telephone to customers.
Established a sincere and trusting rapport while interviewing a variety of candidates across the country for employment.

CUSTOMER SERVICE and PROBLEM SOLVING SKILLS

Assessed and evaluated thoroughly the needs of each customer before suggesting the appropriate product.
Clarified complex concerns and provided clear explanations of the product or service in question to calm troubled customers.
Counseled individuals during their job changes on their wants, desires and needs as well as the consequences of their decisions.

SALES and MARKETING SKILLS

Achieved 140% of quota within the first seven months of selling Yellow Pages advertising.
Persuaded ten individuals to accept new employment during the first year as a personnel recruiter.
Exceeded company goals for ten consecutive months while marketing childrens' books over the telephone.

EMPLOYMENT HISTORY

10/90 - Present	Cole Personnel Co., Inc., Indianapolis, Indiana Executive Recruiter
10/87 - 9/90	Ameritech Publishing Co., Inc., Indianapolis, Indiana Account Executive, Inside Sales
5/85 - 9/87	American Dialing Corporation, Indianapolis, Indiana Account Executive, Inside Sales

PROFESSIONAL AFFILIATIONS and MEMBERSHIPS

Women in Communications, Secretary
Indianapolis Ambassadors, Volunteer

CHRISTOPHER L. WHITE

3130 West Jordan Drive
Indianapolis, Indiana 46220
(317) 844-5052

HIGHLIGHTS OF QUALIFICATIONS

- 16 years successful experience in office products and computer hardware and software systems sales
- Positive motivator, combining creativity with strong verbal and written skills
- Receiver of numerous recognition awards for outstanding achievement as a sales manager and account representative

EDUCATION

Butler University, Indianapolis, Indiana
Bachelor of Arts in English, 1979

EMPLOYMENT HISTORY

8/82–Present   Computer Solutions, Inc., Indianapolis, Indiana

Manager, Strategic Accounts & Specialized Markets   7/90–Present
   Responsible for profitability and marketing efforts within the major account marketplace of Indianapolis. Developed plans to penetrate specific niche vertical markets with the objective of maintaining higher margins through an applications/ solutions sale instead of a pure hardware/software focus. Exceeded margins of 33 points and secured 15 non-profit association headquarters in less than 3 years.

General Manager   1/87–7/90
   Responsible for a systems integration sales and service business with focus on LAN/WAN technologies, database applications, consulting and information management. Implemented sales relationships with major accounts in the target markets of 3 states. Managed a staff of 20 sales, technical and administrative employees generating over $5,000,000 in annual revenue from product sales, consulting and modeling through design, implementation and testing.

Sales Manager   8/82–1/87
   Set up new office for Computer Solutions in Indiana. Recruited and interviewed potential employees. Marketed full line of office automation products to both major accounts and new customers in Central Indiana. Promoted to General Manager based on success as Sales Manager.

Recognition:
   President's Award–1983
   Top Branch Office–1984, 1986, 1987, 1988
   Corporate Revenue Sales Leader–1984, 1985, 1987

6/79–7/82   Phi Beta Alpha General Fraternity, Indianapolis, Indiana

Director of Expansion   7/80–7/82
   Traveled to colleges within the region to discuss the acquisition, programming and installation of new college chapters. Served as liaison to college administrators and spoke to prospective chapters on financial management and group dynamics.

Chapter Consultant   6/79–7/80
   Visited 70 college and university campuses throughout the U.S. and Canada to evaluate and counsel undergraduate officers and alumni on improving chapter operations.

COLLEGE HONORS

Dean's List
Gold Key Honorary
Who's Who in American Colleges & Universities
Fraternity Chapter President
Outstanding Senior
President's Award

Make It a Campaign

A very large percentage of job search campaigns begin and end with these steps:

- Hear about an opportunity
- Mail a resume
- Wait
- Wait
- Wait

It is far more effective to view the job search as a multi-phase campaign. A classic example has become part of the lore of the advertising industry. (We've only slightly fictionalized this true story.)

- In August, the CEO of a large agency receives a wave of postcards announcing "John Miller is Coming."
- In September, the wave of postcards continues "John Miller is Coming on October 6."
- On October 5, a billboard across the street blares "John Miller is coming at 9:30 a.m. on Thursday, October 6."
- At 9:20 on October 6 a delivery truck off-loads a huge crate which is carted into the agency's office.

- While a curious crowd, including the CEO, watches, the sides of the crate are dropped and there, in professional attire, at a mini computer workstation, sits John Miller.
- He was hired on the spot.

While perhaps an extreme example, John's approach makes clear that a distinctive job search campaign can and should include multiple elements.

At a minimum we suggest:
- Initial resume/cover letter mailing.
- Almost immediate follow-up by phone or a clever mailing to attempt to move the resume to the top of the stack.
- Appropriate thank you's for:
  —Speaking with me by phone;
  —Meeting with me;
  —Meeting with me for a second interview.
- Printed elements of the campaign having a distinctive look and/or theme which is included in every piece.

Aggressive follow-up is certainly consistent with the Edge strategy. A resume sitting in a pile of 400 may need an extra boost to reach the top of the stack, so these kinds of ideas will be helpful:

By Phone:
Opinions are divided about aggressively following up by phone. Some job seekers don't do it simply because they are totally uncomfortable with the process. Others, particularly those seeking jobs in the fields of sales and marketing, view personal contact as a natural part of selling themselves. In these fields, failure to follow-up might be construed as lack of critical aggressiveness.

Consider the following examples:

"It is far more effective to view the job search as a multi-phase campaign."

- "Frank, this is Jerome Mitchell. I'm applying for your job in payables. It really looks like my background fits your needs perfectly. I don't want to be overly pushy, but I'll be in your area Tuesday and wondered if I might stop by to meet with you briefly."
- "Mr. Jones, this is Fred Johnson. Our mutual friend Jim Jackson told me about your opening in sales and thought my background as a 14-year veteran of sales management would be perfect. Might I stop by for a few minutes to discuss the possibility?"
- "Miss Marshall, this is Peggy McConnell. I know your formal application system is probably by mail, but I'm so excited about the opportunity you're offering I wanted to call and see if I could arrange an interview. Your job fits my skills exactly. Would you be willing to see me for a few minutes?"

In Person:

Even more aggressive than a phone call is simply showing up at the target office. At worst you can drop off a resume. With luck, some discussion with the person in the reception office, and perhaps a bit of dancing and singing, you might wrangle a brief interview.
- "Mary, I know Mr. Smith is busy and he may insist on prior appointments, but do you suppose there's any chance he'd see me for a couple minutes?"
- "I was so excited about the job opportunity you advertised in the Journal that I drove over as fast as possible. I really think I'd be perfect for that job! Is there any chance I might speak with someone about it while I'm here?"
- (If in a smaller business and you can actually see a decision maker) "I realize I don't have an appointment, but I really think I'd be perfect for the job you're advertising. Could we spend a couple minutes discussing it?"
- (If visiting even though not aware of a specific job opening) "I wonder if I might fill out an application and leave my resume... Do you suppose someone would be willing to speak with me for a couple minutes about possible future job opportunities?..." (If you spot an apparent decision maker) "My name is Mary Smith. I'm in the job

market which is certainly tough right now. I know you probably don't have any immediate openings, but would you be willing to spend 5 minutes sharing some ideas on how someone like me should approach the job market?"

Certainly there is no guarantee that visiting will lead to an interview, but the strategy is as old as selling. If you are pleasant and professional and you ask enough people, you'll eventually find a person who just learned that a key employee is leaving or a person who has been halfway thinking about a new hire, or even a person who respects your moxie and will spend a few minutes with you.

Unconventional Mail Follow-up:
Only the imagination limits the number of methods of recontacting a target company. At its most basic, you simply develop a set of letters or cards designed strictly to keep your name in front of the decision maker. For example:

- "In reflecting further on your job opportunity, I became even more convinced that my abilities fit your needs. During my 3 years at ABC Corp., I created 24 new accounts of the type your company is seeking. My resume may not make clear the extent to which our new client program fits your objectives. I am excited about pursuing this opportunity and look forward to hearing from you soon."
- "My resume is presently on file with you. I worked hard to keep it to one page, but in reflecting on your job opportunity, I realized that an experience I had in the mid '80s was very relevant..."

"Aggressive follow-up is certainly consistent with the Edge strategy."

- (If your experience is limited versus other likely candidates) "I woke up this morning with the really bad feeling that my resume may not be on the top of your stack. I know there are other applicants with a longer list of jobs, but I truly feel you'll be making the right decision if you give me an interview. I know enough to come down running in the job. What I don't know immediately I'll learn quickly. And you'll never find someone who will work harder to make the job and your company successful... Thanks, in advance, for your consideration."

Many applicants orchestrate a campaign including as many as three follow-up mailings, a phone call, and appropriate "thank you" mailings after the interviews. Examples of less conventional mail follow-up include:

- Create a truly unusual version of your resume. The following chapter carries ideas, but one good example is a resume blown up to 17" x 22", four times normal size, forwarded with a note such as, "Knowing that resumes struggle to be noticed in today's job market, I thought I'd forward one almost certain to stand out. Seriously, my conventional resume was forwarded last week, and I'm sure it will receive whatever attention it deserves. I did want you to know that I may be a little more creative than the average applicant, and I really am excited about working for your company. Thanks in advance for your consideration..."
- We've already mentioned our associate who got his foot in the door by forwarding one of his shoes via UPS. His note said "I've been trying for months to get my foot in your door, so decided to try another approach. I truly believe my qualifications are ideal for your company. A resume is enclosed..."
- Inspired by our associate's shoe, The Edge has created a diecut foot, virtually life-size and complete with toe nails and other details, which can be mailed with a note similar to the one above. See Appendix B for details.
- A follow-up letter can include something unique such as a gag reference list with testimonials.

"He certainly knows how to save pennies so his company increases earnings." —Benjamin Franklin

"He works harder to develop good ideas than I did when I invented the lightbulb." —Thomas Edison

The list should include some quotations from recognized historical figures in the industry, a subtle way to demonstrate knowledge.

Utilizing the unusual can certainly fulfill the goal of having your application become a "keeper." It is CERTAIN, that a person who receives a foot or a giant resume will react strongly. If they're the kind of people who react positively to initiative and creativity, you have leapt ahead of competitive applications.

Whether using the usual or unusual, the follow-up concept completes your job search strategy. You have a resume, a tailored cover letter, and a pre-planned set of follow-up steps. As you relentlessly execute this strategy, good things are much more likely to happen.

Also note the importance of becoming aware of the target company's hiring procedure. Many companies, particularly large businesses, have a multi-step process which may include:

- Pre-screening to 40 applicants by a Human Resources clerk;
- Pre-screening to 15 applicants by a Human Resources manager;
- Screening to 6 interviewees by the working manager;
- First interview for the top 6;
- Second interview for the top 3.

If you can understand this process in advance, learn names of key people, execute follow-up with the right people along the way, your odds increase dramatically.

The other extreme is a small company in which the entrepreneur is also the personnel department. He is likely very busy. His hiring system is something like this:

- Scan the resume stack.
- Find 3 or 4 that look good.

- Call 'em in.
- Hire the first who really seems to fit the need.

In Job Market 90s, a very large percentage of job openings are being created in the small business sector. Fortunately, the entire Edge concept fits extremely well with a small business, entrepreneurial mentality which tends to appreciate initiative and creativity.

Every element of our book can be brought to bear in this kind of job search:

- Research of available opportunities can be conducted by aggressively reading and networking;
- Once an attractive company is found, research can continue at two specific levels:
  — The company's business situation and needs;
  — The CEO's individual background, style, and interests.
- A unique campaign will likely be noticed and appreciated.
- It is possible to directly approach the CEO with suggestions such as: "I am confident I'm your person for this manufacturing job. Let me visit your company at my own expense for two days. I'll just observe; then give you a report on my observations and recommendations. I believe you'll see I have the kind of knowledge and skills you're looking for. If not, I'm history."

"Only the imagination limits the number of methods of recontacting a target company."

CHAPTER 12

Moving Even Closer to the Edge

It is ironic for three reasons that the world of traditional resumes is dry, factual and gray:

1. As we've stressed throughout this book, your dry, factual, gray resume has little chance of standing out in a huge crowd.

2. A survey of bosses rated "sense of humor" as the most important single quality in their employees. Yet resumes rarely exhibit this key trait.

3. The poor soul who must read 400 resumes faces deadly boredom. Some bright spots will be appreciated simply because they break the routine.

Again, a resume can stand out by simple devices such as adding color. If you are confident your words—both resume content and cover letter—make it clear you are an outstanding candidate, you need not consider using more extreme approaches. Even in this case, however, use of some relaxed humor can communicate both confidence and sense of humor:

- "It must be an incredible job reading through the stack of resumes you'll receive for this position. I'd like to think this one can save you some time. When I read your list of qualifications, I said 'John, this is the job you've spent 15 years getting ready for.'..."

- "When I see an interesting career opportunity, I always make a 2-column list: What You Want...What I Offer. The job you listed on Sunday fit so well I almost addressed this letter to 'Dear Glove:' Seriously, I am excited

about the fit. I believe my resume will indicate the extent to which I am ready to tackle this position. And I look forward to the opportunity to meet with you..."
(As an idea closer to the Edge, you could use similar wording and enclose a glove).

This chapter is intended for those who make this critical assessment: These people are going to receive 500 resumes. There is no chance that my pedigree will be in the top 3%. Relying strictly on my words, I will never emerge from the deep stack. Therefore, I have nothing to lose and much to gain by daring to be different.

Note that this assessment is NOT an indication that you are calling yourself a loser or are otherwise negative about your self-worth. You are simply saying:

- I've not been in the work force nearly as long as many other applicants. Their list of credentials will be far longer than mine; or
- I've worked for a relatively unknown company and will be competing with candidates from more prestigious firms; or
- These people value Ivy League education highly and, unfortunately, my degree is from Podunk State; or
- I'm trying to jump from one industry to another; therefore, my credentials will not appear as relevant as those who have spent their careers in the industry.

Moreover, you are not saying you're becoming a con person who will use gimmicks to get a job. You're simply saying: "I am confident I can do this job if given a chance. I am a unique person with creativity. Why not demonstrate that creativity while creating a resume package so unique that I'll at least be noticed?"

"A survey of bosses rated sense of humor as one of the most important single qualities in their employees. Yet resumes rarely exhibit this key trait."

The balance of this chapter carries ideas of all kinds. We suggest you read through the chapter a couple of times and go to the place (shower or wherever) where your most creative ideas come to you. Or, perhaps by recruiting people you enjoy brainstorming with, you can adapt an approach which is right for you.

Some of the ideas may require working with a graphic artist. However, all can be executed easily using desktop publishing along with basic drawings or clip art. (Various clip art is presented in Appendix B.)

Resume Concepts Closer To The Edge:
(some shown in thumbnails)

- Simulate computer paper with holes and perforations printed at the sides of the resume.
- Print a computer with giant screen on the resume (or cover letter). Put words inside the screen as if they had been word-processed onto the screen.
- Create separate pieces such as a briefcase, suitcase, miniature dollar bills, miniature contracts, or other designs relevant to your profession. Glue those pieces onto the resume or cover letter.
  - *"I realize the job involves heavy travel throughout the eastern seaboard. My suitcase is packed and ready..."*
  - *"I know my marketing skills will lead to many important contracts for your firm..."*
- Utilize the concept of a seed becoming a sprout becoming a full grown plant or tree.
- Find a picture of yourself as a child doing something related to the position. Caption it: "From an early age, in training to..."
- Consider a completely separate page for your unique idea (such as the child picture). Making the resume package:
  - Cover letter (including reference to page 2 as a demonstration of creativity);
  - Creative page
  - Resume

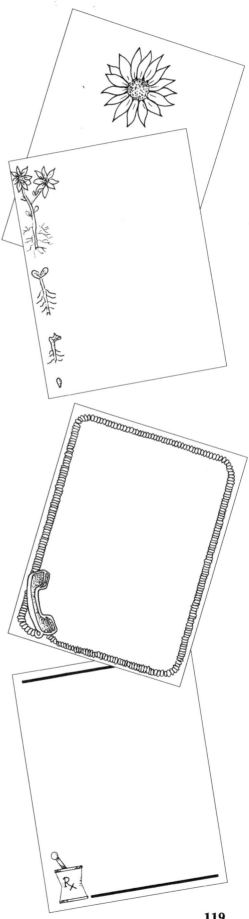

The creative page could include...

- Cartoons
- A gag list of famous people in the field with your name sandwiched between Thomas Watson and Steven Jobs
- A gag set of endorsements or references including famous people, living and dead, and relatives...

  "This lady knows about savings and earnings; dollars not just pennies." —Benjamin Franklin

  "She is hardworking, bright and alert. Definitely a wonderful person for your job position." —Her mother

- A photo of an old-fashioned sports team or of a team you formerly played on with caption such as: "Aware of the importance of dedication, hard work, teamwork."
- A simulated newspaper front page carrying "stories" about your career. *(See page 14.)*

Other Resume Ideas:

- A printed target in the background of the resume and/or cover letter with words suggesting they'll be on target when they hire you. (Requires a printing process called "screening" onto a metal plate. We suggest a 10% screen tint.) Target could be printed in a color, probably red which will make the result very pale red when printed.
- The concept of a missing link. Cover letter printed with a chain across bottom, one link missing. Resume printed with that link at top.
- A tiny version of your resume, perhaps 4 x 6. Clip it to the cover letter with words such as "Throughout my career, I have relentlessly sought ways to improve profitability through reducing cost. My mini-resume indicates this dedication. However, realizing it's a bit hard to read, I've also enclosed a full-size version." (This can probably be accomplished on desktop equipment by printing at a reduced percentage. If not legible, a printer can make a "PMT reduction" which will provide legibility at tiny size.)
- Also, for those demonstrating cost-cutting orientation, print the back of the resume and cover letter with something indicating the paper has already been used and you

are recycling the back side. One sheet could be a memo from a fellow employee, the other a handwritten note from a relative. Words would stress your constant orientation toward cost reduction.

- A jumbo resume, perhaps 17"x22". This will fold in fourths to fit a 9x12 envelope. Use language such as, "Knowing that the person you seek must be willing to think big to be successful, I hereby show my willingness! Also, for your convenience, I've enclosed a standard version."

- A distinctive logo of your own, perhaps initials built into an industry symbol, which appears on all your material: envelope, cover letter, resume, follow-up card.

- If working with a strong commercial printer, discuss possible use of these techniques:

  — *Varnish (transparent ink which creates a shiny area where it's printed.) This technique creates subtle highlighting and could be used wherever you want special emphasis.*

  — *Embossing (creating raised or depressed areas on the sheet, perhaps for a monogram or industry symbol).*

- Forward your resume padded to the top of perhaps 20 sheets of plain paper. When resume is torn off, reader will have a usable notepad. Explain that you wanted to be sure your resume was at the top of the stack.

- Print a real or simulated thumbprint with wording about your uniqueness.

- Send a version of your resume cut into perhaps 5 pieces to create a puzzle. Wording such as "I'm confident I can solve the 'who to hire' puzzle."

- Use the puzzle idea as a follow-up device. Follow your more traditional resume with a resume cut into pieces. Include a note such as "I continue to be confident I can solve your 'who to hire' puzzle. (Actually, my intact version was forwarded three days ago, but I just wanted to stay in touch!) I look forward to hearing from you..."

- Follow up by sending an actual shoe or diecut foot indicating your attempt to "get your foot in the door." (Refer to Chapter 11.)

- If applying for a position in sales or marketing, use the

idea of getting a person to sign their name on the dotted line. For example, in your cover letter you could write: "I am so oriented toward getting clients to sign on the dotted line, I couldn't help including this concept in my resume. Please sign below..." At the bottom of the page would be something like:

Yes, this applicant definitely deserves further consideration.

Signed_____

- Include a blank post-it note or a post-it note already carrying the line "Excellent candidate, be sure to inter-view" attached to your resume or cover letter with words such as, "I'm so confident of the fit between your needs and my qualifications, I've taken the liberty of enclosing a post-it note for your use."
- If money is no object and you're connected in the field of high-end graphic design, consider some kind of pop-up resume.
- Utilize a resume in completely different format, for example, a traditional brochure format.
- If the envelope is likely to be seen by the decision-maker, include art or slogans on the envelope:

"Resume of an excellent candidate trapped in here—please release and review!"

Video Resumes:

Television provides a relatively new medium for resumes.
- Your own video tape, whether home-produced or professionally produced.
- Participation in a video job exchange—an emerging trend on cable channels in various cities.

Two considerations are vital...
- Your research must indicate that the video will be viewed.
- Your candid self-assessment must confirm that you project well via TV.

Writing a Resume

The Edge resume system makes a distinction between (1) the basic writing of a resume and (2) the design and presentation of that resume. Previous chapters have stressed uniqueness of APPROACH. However, a jokester's comment about a popular book is very appropriate here: "It doesn't matter what color your parachute is if it doesn't open." No amount of clever presentation will overcome a poorly organized, poorly written resume.

We present this chapter for those either starting the resume writing process or those willing to take a hard look at their present resume. Frankly, a large percentage of current resumes are seriously flawed: poorly organized, too long, too short, misdirected in terms of emphasis, or incorrect in terms of grammar and spelling.

There are, however, two potential reasons for skipping this chapter:

- If your resume is current and unquestionably well-crafted, there is no need to reinvent the wheel. You might browse this section for new ideas. But your use of the Edge will involve unique presentation of your words.
- You may want to consult other books, or work directly with resume-writing experts. Without question, there are professional resume consultants who have excellent approaches to word-crafting. We are gratified that many of these professionals have embraced our concept, realizing that in today's competitive marketplace, an Edge is necessary; and that our approach is compatible with, not competitive with, their role as professionals. At your local library, there may be as many as 100 books dealing with resume writing. Again, many of these books are excellent sources. We have listed several leading books at the end of this section.

For those preferring to utilize this reference book, we present a compilation of the resume writing concepts which seem helpful and necessary.

A Quick Word about Writer's Block

Professional writers occasionally experience a strange paralysis known as writer's block. For some reason, the words just won't come. The words that do come are not the words you want. And the waste basket (electronic or metal) is soon full of discarded starts. A variation of this malady often attacks the resume writer. You find it very hard to decide which experiences are most relevant. You find it hard to find a balance between confidently presenting your skills and sounding like a braggart. You have trouble deciding how much to tailor the resume to specific job possibilities. So you struggle.

Realize that this agony is experienced by virtually every resume writer. It is one of the key reasons to consider utilizing professional help. Those going-it-alone often find the best approach is:

- Try it today;
- Sleep on it overnight;
- Be prepared to make major edits of your own work and

try for draft 2;
- And so on, until complete.

In summary, it is not at all likely that you'll create your final draft in one or even two writing sessions.

Resume Formats

Perusal of most resume writing books can lead to the terrifying conclusion that there are 101 formats from which to choose. Actually there are only three basic formats:
- Chronological
- Functional
- Combination of functional/chronological

The following pages include a sample of each along with discussion of its primary purposes.

Chronological

The chronological resume is a virtual time line, plotting your education and career in reverse chronological order. Some of the people reading resumes have apparently attended a course called "Investigative Resume Reading" where they learned to "find gaps" in applicants' experiences. Occasionally, no doubt, they uncover a prison term or other career embarrassment; but we suspect the exercise is just one way to add a bit of structure to the very subjective job of resume review. In any case, it is important enough that most resumes should account for the majority of our adult years on earth.

Obviously, the chronological resume is the simplest format to meet this objective.

From the standpoint of the resume writer, this format is most applicable if:

- Your career path demonstrates a set of experiences directly relevant to the position being pursued;
- The progression of your career shows the kind of steady advancement which indicates you are a career winner;
- The number of positions held and the number of career jumps is appropriate at this stage of your career.

Reversing the logic: if your experience isn't directly relevant to the position being pursued or your career hasn't progressed logically or you have hopscotched all over the industry, the chronological format is almost certainly not best.

Whatever the resume format, but particularly if using a chronological format, remember to stress accomplishments instead of simply printing your job description. Programs implemented, problems solved, and numbers achieved are the kinds of information which sell your talent.

Functional

The functional resume places its emphasis on experiences relevant to the position you are pursuing (e.g. supervision, quality control, public relations, marketing, communication, computer programming). There is much less emphasis on dates.

Your employment history is still important in this format, but you will place it near the end of your resume. Simply list the dates, employer names and positions held.

"Some of the people reading resumes have apparently attended a course called Investigative Resume Reading..."

You will not detail your responsibilities in that part of the resume.

The functional resume is very common in difficult job markets because of the likely need to make significant career adjustments. For some, these adjustments involve convincing someone in another industry that your skills are transferable. Others are attempting jumps into new job categories. In either case, the chronological resume is almost certainly inappropriate. You must stress the skills you possess, communicating in such a way that it is clear your skills are transferable to the new situation.

Combination

The combination resume typically begins as a functional resume by listing those significant skills which are pertinent to obtaining the position you desire. The following section lists companies for which you have worked in reverse chronological order. However, in a combination resume, responsibilities and achievements are listed for each position.

This resume format is the choice of upwardly mobile professionals who are on the fast track in a particular career or industry, demonstrating both skills and a successful career track. Typically, the format is not used by those having less than 12-15 years in the workforce.

SAMPLE—CHRONOLOGICAL FORMAT

MICHAEL E. OLSON
4748 East 84th Street
New York, New York 10036
(212) 674-0090

SUMMARY OF QUALIFICATIONS

- Outstanding track record of marketing accomplishments including: product development, new market penetration and advertising and sales promotion.
- Widely experienced in profit and loss, training and supervision, and public relations.
- Creator of numerous and successful telemarketing, direct mail and trade show exhibit programs.
- Results-oriented executive combining problem-solving analytical skills with a strong creative flair.

CAREER HISTORY

OMNICOM, *New York, New York*
Director, Market Research, *April 1988—Present*

Major Clients: Gillette, Polaroid, Du Pont, Avon, Walgreens, General Electric, Pillsbury, Holiday Inn

- Established and directed all facilities of agency's marketing research department. Successfully developed the marketing research function into a profit center.
- Interpreted marketing research and recommendations to improve the quality of client decision making.
- Developed a new approach to reporting and interpreting consumer change for management.

BAUSCH & LOMB, NEW PRODUCTS DIVISION, *Rochester, New York*
Marketing Manager, *May 1983—March 1988*

- Conceptualized new product designs in current product which were adopted by management, yielding increased sales of $115,000.
- Introduced product line to new market segments, resulting in multiple purchases and a $300,000 improvement in sales.
- Created and facilitated product seminars for customers and prospects.
- Coordinated and conducted training of sales representatives and managers, leading to $376,000 increase in sales.

PREMARK INTERNATIONAL, HOUSEHOLD PRODUCTS DIVISION, *Deerfield, Illinois*
Marketing Research Services Manager, *May 1979—April 1983*
Marketing Research Brand Manager, *July 1975—April 1979*

- Planned and conducted all marketing research for new consumer household products from idea conception through test market.
- Initiated new products team approach by successfully collaborating with members of virtually every corporate group while conducting several new product projects at various stages of development.
- Hired and trained a research assistant and set up a research library.

EDUCATION

Columbia University, *New York, New York*
M.B.A., Marketing, 1990

University of Illinois, *Champagne, Illinois*
B.B.A., Marketing, 1975

SAMPLE—FUNCTIONAL FORMAT

HELEN M. YOUNG
3003 North Lincoln Avenue
Indianapolis, IN 46208
(317) 279-7900

AREAS OF ACHIEVEMENT

Public Relations
Coordinated and established an Information/Media Center in the Republic of the Philippines. Initiated and wrote press releases, answered queries and directed photo opportunities.

Provided positive publicity in Japan for the American community on nationwide and local Japanese television.

Established ongoing working rapport with the American Embassy and the International Press Center in Japan and the Republic of the Philippines.

Communications
Initiated on-camera media training for CEOs.

Spoke for the Navy in Washington, D.C. concerning a wide variety of issues with leading national and international media representatives. Participated on an education steering committee related to an HIV/AIDS education film to be distributed Navy-wide.

Developed and executed comprehensive training programs from concept to delivery. Instructed 2,000 U.S. and foreign public relations students annually in the area of public relations, media relations, internal information, electronic news, gathering, editing and planning.

Arranged, organized and conducted tours, sporting events and social function for the internal audience, general public and media representatives in 12 countries with participation ranging from 2 to 12,000.

Management
Supervised the daily performance of four separate public relations offices which solved public relations problems in the U.S. and overseas.

Prepared the budgets for five different offices.

Recruited and trained over 55 employees.

Coordinated purchasing for offices of 75 staff.

EMPLOYMENT HISTORY

1988-Present   Assistant Professor
Defense Information School, Fort Benjamin Harrison, Indianapolis, Indiana

1984-1987   Public Affairs Officer
Navy Bureau of Medicine & Surgery, Washington, D.C.

1982-1983   Media Officer
Bureau of Navy Information, The Pentagon, Washington, D.C.

1980-1981   Director—Speakers Bureau
Bureau of Navy Information, The Pentagon, Washington, D.C.

1975-1979   Public Affairs Officer
Naval Security Group Activity, Misawa, Japan

EDUCATION

Butler University, *Indianapolis, Indiana*
Master of Arts, Communication, 1975

University of Illinois, *Champaign, Illinois*
Bachelor of Science, Public Relations, 1973

CERTIFICATES OF COMPLETION

Defense Information School, *Indianapolis, Indiana*
- *Public Affairs Officer Course, 1975*
- *Electronic News Gathering & Editing Techniques, 1975*
- *Television Production, 1975*

SAMPLE—COMBINATION FORMAT

LAURA DOBBS

8565 North Oak Street
Indianapolis, Indiana 46260
(317) 844-6500

SUMMARY

- Fifteen years accounting experience with a strong background in auditing, business and individual taxes and cost control programs.
- Excellent management skills. Consistently obtain high productivity from employees.
- Efficient in implementing computerized accounting systems and designing more effective manual systems.
- Rapidly recognize and analyze company problems and solutions.

EDUCATION

Certified Public Accountant, 1980
Indiana State Certification

Indiana University, Bloomington, Indiana
Bachelor of Science, 1977
Major: Accounting; *Minor:* Business Administration

PROFESSIONAL EXPERIENCE

Cost Accounting
- Developed a major cost control program that cut overhead 15%.
- Reduced costs for small businesses and large corporations.
- Established complete integrated accounting package for entire corporations.

Accounting and Budgeting
- Designed, installed and implemented effective budgeting systems under cash and accrual accounting methods.
- Established accounting procedures which significantly reduced errors and duplication of effort by 55%.
- Tracked and reduced costs for multi-million dollar contracts.

Auditing
- Performed audits and developed financial statements for a wide variety of clients.
- Audited multi-million dollar subcontractors accounting records and facilities for government contracts.
- Trained employees to comply with new state accounting regulations and identified accounting and operational irregularities.

Management and Administration
- Hired, trained and managed 5-40 employees.
- Set up and conducted monthly motivational staff meetings.
- Extensively involved in customer relations, establishing credit ratings, approving credit, reviewing and approving customer claims and making collections.

EMPLOYMENT HISTORY

1988-Present *Controller,* **Indiana Bell,** *Indianapolis, Indiana*
Developed a major cost control program that cut overhead 15%. Trained employees to comply with new state accounting regulations and identified accounting and operations irregularities.

1981-1988 *Controller,* **Cummins Engine,** *Columbus, Indiana*
Established complete integrated accounting package for entire corporation. Developed accounting procedures which reduced errors and duplication of effort by 55%.

1977-1981 *Staff Accountant,* **Arthur Andersen & Co.,** *Indianapolis, Indiana*
Converted manual accounting systems to efficient computerized office systems for several companies in Indianapolis. Designed, installed and implemented effective budgeting systems under cash and accrual accounting methods.

"A Rose by Any Other Name..."

In the interest of presenting a more complete work regarding resume writing, we briefly cover the subject of properly presenting your name. Seriously, there are some issues to keep in mind.

Normally, it looks and works best to state your first name, middle initial and last name (e.g. Susan J. Miller). An exception arises for those whose parents gave them a first name which they have long since ducked (like Winfield). In this case, the resume may appropriately read "W. Scott Montgomery."

Even if your friends call you Susie or Bill or Jack, it is usually better to use only the formal name "Susan J. Miller" rather that Susie Miller or Susan "Susie" J. Miller. An exception might be a person well enough known in the industry to have a recognized nickname: Babe Ruth surely didn't use George Herman Ruth on his resume.

In most cases, it's best to have no more than one initial in the name. Susan J. is almost certainly better than S. J. Miller. It is usually unnecessary to write out your full name (e.g. Susan Joan Miller).

Be aware that married women may wish to include their maiden names to more easily facilitate reference checking (e.g. Mary (Johnson) McCoy). If you feel that the use of a hyphenated last name will make some kind of impression on your reader, then consult with friends and advisors on the likely impact.

Telephone Numbers

Since an offer to interview is rarely granted by mail, it is imperative that you include your full telephone number on the line below your address. Ideally you should list day and evening numbers, but all resume readers are aware that your job search may be confidential and a "work number" may not be practical.

Dates

Any of several formats can be used for presenting dates. The most important issue is consistency throughout your resume.

January 1988 - December 1991
January 2, 1988 - December 31, 1991
1/88 - 12/91
1/2/88 - 12/31/91

Objectives

Resume books agonize at length over whether to state an objective and, if so, how.

Resume readers chuckle at transparent attempts of writers to construct an objective which sounds like your lifelong dream has been to work in Acme Manufacturing's Computer Department.

Resume printers smile all the way to the bank when resume writers print three different versions of their resume, different only in the statement of objective.

This advice seems safe. If an objective sounds fluffy along these lines:

OBJECTIVE: To become part of a dynamic company which appreciates and rewards excellent effort.

OBJECTIVE: To obtain a challenging position with a progressive company that can use my experiences and my liberal arts education.

OBJECTIVE: To obtain a challenging position with a progressive company that can offer me the opportunity for advancement.

...skip it

Similarly, if you are obviously applying for a job in the public relations department of a dynamic company, it seems unnecessary to state:

OBJECTIVE: To contribute positively to the public relations effort of a dynamic company

In almost every case, a far better way to accomplish the purpose of the objective is coverage in the cover letter, e.g. "I am seeking an opportunity to grow in the field of public relations and feel confident there is an excellent fit between your needs and my skills..."

After having read hundreds of resumes and having spoken to many hiring authorities, we have learned that the majority of individuals in this job market are opting to omit an objective.

Two exceptions should be considered. If an objective is so clear that it shows a carefully thought-out career path which fits perfectly with the position, it might be considered:

OBJECTIVE: To utilize my experience in turnaround management as CEO of a struggling company willing to reward me for specific results.

OBJECTIVE: To utilize my 15 years experience in marketing and computer systems design to become Sales Manager of a major software company.

(Note, however, that even these objectives can be covered as well or better in the cover letter.)

Those interested in differentiating their resume by the use of Edge humor can certainly use the objective for this purpose:

OBJECTIVE: To get a better job so my wife gets off my back.

OBJECTIVE: Getting someone to realize that my skills are great, my work ethic is excellent, and I'm the ideal person for this job.

Summary

A summary is a listing of three to five highlights of your achievements and qualifications that should precede your work history or functional skills. Because your resume is likely to be in heavy competition for attention, the summary is excellent as a means of grabbing attention and inspiring the reader to carefully review the rest of your qualifications.

Typical SUMMARIES might be:
- Effective problem solver using excellent written and verbal communication skills.
- Excellent track record for generating overall cost reduction and operation efficiency improvements.
- M.B.A. from Indiana University in Business Management.
- Strong leadership skills while advancing a team player approach.

- 10 years as a proven sales leader with an excellent record of achievement.
- Confident, professional communicator with outstanding presentation skills.
- Special talent for identifying clients' needs and presenting effective solutions.
- Dependable, flexible and able to maintain a sense of humor under pressure.
- Successfully managed budgets in excess of $2 million.
- Outstanding management skills while overseeing more than 60 employees.
- Experienced in developing short- and long-term financial business planning.
- Positive motivator, combining creativity with strong verbal and writing skills.

Here is a list of powerful words and phrases that will describe the qualities you may want to emphasize in your summary or anywhere in your resume.

ABILITY TO...	EFFICIENT	PROBLEM SOLVER
ACCOMPLISHED IN...	ENERGETIC	PROFESSIONAL
ACCURATE	ENTHUSIASTIC	PROFICIENT
ACHIEVED	EXCELLENT	PROFITABLY
ADEPT	EXCEPTIONAL	PROVEN
AGGRESSIVE	EXPERIENCED	QUICK
ANALYTICAL	EXTENSIVE	READILY
ASSERTIVE	EXTREMELY	RESPONSIBLE
ATTENTION TO DETAIL	FLEXIBLE	RELIABLE
CHALLENGING	FOLLOW THROUGH	SELF-MOTIVATED
COMMITTED TO...	TO COMPLETION	SENSE OF HUMOR
COMMUNICATION SKILLS	GOAL ACHIEVER	SHARP
COMPETENT	HIGHLY	SPECIAL TALENT
COMPETITIVE	INDUSTRIOUS	STRONG
CONSISTENT	INTERPERSONAL SKILLS	SUCCESSFUL
CREATIVE	KNOWLEDGEABLE	TACTFUL
DEDICATED TO...	LEADERSHIP	TAKE DIRECTIONS
DECISIVE	LEARN QUICKLY	TEAM PLAYER
DEMONSTRATED	MEET DEADLINES	THOROUGH
DEPENDABLE	MOTIVATED	THRIVE ON...
DETAIL ORIENTED	OBJECTIVE	TRUST
DILIGENT	ORGANIZED	UNDER PRESSURE
DIPLOMATIC	ORIGINAL	UNDERSTANDING
EASILY	OUTSTANDING	UNIQUE
EFFECTIVE	POSITIVE ATTITUDE	VERSATILE

Skills and Experience

Communicating skills and experience involves questions of both writing skills and personal integrity.

It is certainly true that your resume will be in competition with some written by skillful workers and others written by skillful fibbers. It is crucial that you put the best possible light on your accomplishments. However, staying within the bounds of truthfulness is wise.

Some people who "directed the activity of 150 people" were simply chairman of the company picnic committee. Boldfaced puffery is likely to backfire but these concepts are important.

- Describe your successes and accomplishments with creativity and confidence.
- Avoid simply listing your duties as if you were writing a company job description for your boss.
- Avoid any negative words or descriptions.
- Avoid using industry jargon and flowery words the reader may not understand.
- Incorporate numbers, percentages and statistics into your descriptions when you can.
- Keep your sentences short. Be brief and to the point. Many resumes contain lengthy, convoluted sentences which sound like intentional mumbo-jumbo.
- Avoid using the pronoun "I." Write in abbreviated third person (e.g. Instead of writing "I recruited, trained and coordinated activities of 10,000 volunteers," try writing "Recruited, trained and coordinated activities of 10,000 volunteers."
- Use action verbs to describe your skills and achievements. Here is a list of proven action verbs:

"Because your resume is likely to be in heavy competition for attention, the summary is excellent as a means of grabbing attention."

ACCELERATED	ACCOMPLISHED	ACHIEVED	ACTED
ADAPTED	ADDED	ADDRESSED	ADMINISTERED
ADVANCED	ADVISED	ALLOCATED	ANALYZED
APPRAISED	APPROVED	ARRANGED	ASSEMBLED
ASSIGNED	ASSISTED	ATTAINED	AUDITED
AUTHORED	AUTOMATED	BALANCED	BROADENED
BUDGETED	BUILT	CALCULATED	CATALOGUED
CHANGED	CHAIRED	CLARIFIED	CLASSIFIED
COACHED	COLLECTED	COMPILED	COMPLETED
COMPOSED	COMPUTED	CONCEIVED	CONCEPTUALIZED
CONDUCTED	CONFERRED	CONFRONTED	CONSOLIDATED
CONSTRUCTED	CONTRACTED	CONTRIBUTED	CONTROLLED
CONVERTED	COORDINATED	CORRESPONDED	COUNSELED
CREATED	CRITIQUED	CUT	DECIDED
DECREASED	DELEGATED	DELIVERED	DEMONSTRATED
DERIVED	DESIGNED	DETERMINED	DEVELOPED
DEVISED	DIRECTED	DISPATCHED	DISPENSED
DISPLAYED	DISTINGUISHED	DISTRIBUTED	DIVERSIFIED
DOUBLED	DRAFTED	DRAMATIZED	EARNED
EDITED	EDUCATED	EFFECTED	ELIMINATED
ENABLED	ENCOURAGED	ENGINEERED	ENLISTED
ESTIMATED	ESTABLISHED	EVALUATED	EXAMINED
EXECUTED	EXHIBITED	EXPANDED	EXPEDITED
EXPLAINED	EXPRESSED	EXTRACTED	FABRICATED
FACILITATED	FAMILIARIZED	FASHIONED	FOCUSED
FORECASTED	FORMULATED	FOUNDED	GAINED
GENERATED	GUIDED	HALVED	HANDLED
IDENTIFIED	ILLUSTRATED	IMAGINED	IMPLEMENTED
IMPROVED	INCREASED	INDOCTRINATED	INFLUENCED
INFORMED	INITIATED	INNOVATED	INSPECTED
INSTALLED	INSTITUTED	INSTRUCTED	INTEGRATED
INTERPRETED	INTERVIEWED	INTRODUCED	INVENTED
INVESTIGATED	LAUNCHED	LECTURED	LED
LOCATED	MADE	MAINTAINED	MANAGED
MARKETED	MEASURED	MEDIATED	MODERATED
MONITORED	MOTIVATED	NARRATED	NEGOTIATED
OPERATED	ORGANIZED	ORIGINATED	OVERHAULED
OVERSAW	PARTICIPATED	PERFORMED	PERSUADED
PINPOINTED	PLANNED	PREDICTED	PREPARED
PRESENTED	PRIORITIZED	PROCESSED	PRODUCED
PROGRAMMED	PROJECTED	PROMOTED	PROPOSED
PROVIDED	PUBLICIZED	PUBLISHED	PURCHASED
RAISED	REALIZED	RECOMMENDED	RECONCILED
RECORDED	RECRUITED	REDESIGNED	REDUCED
REFERRED	REGULATED	REHABILITATED	REINFORCED
REMODELED	REORGANIZED	REPAIRED	REPRESENTED
RESEARCHED	RESOLVED	RESTORED	RESTRUCTURED
RETRIEVED	REVAMPED	REVERSED	REVIEWED
REVISED	REVITALIZED	SAVED	SCHEDULED
SCREENED	SELECTED	SERVED	SERVICED
SHAPED	SIMPLIFIED	SKETCHED	SKILLED
SOLD	SOLIDIFIED	SOLVED	SPARKED
SPOKE	SPECIFIED	STAFFED	STARTED
STIMULATED	STRATEGIZED	STREAMLINED	STRENGTHENED
STRESSED	STRETCHED	STRUCTURED	SUCCEEDED
SUMMARIZED	SUPERVISED	SURVEYED	SYSTEMIZED
TABULATED	TAUGHT	TESTED	TRACED
TRACKED	TRAINED	TRANSFERRED	TRANSFORMED
TRANSLATED	TRAVELED	TRIMMED	TURNED
UNCOVERED	UNIFIED	UPDATED	UPGRADED
UTILIZED	VALIDATED	VERIFIED	VISUALIZED
WIDENED	WON	WORKED	

Education

Knowing where to place your education depends on many factors: your years of experience, your level of education and the relevance of your education to the position you are pursuing. Regardless of the degrees you have attained, you will always list them in reverse chronological order. College graduates need not list high school graduation unless graduation is very recent and there is limited relevant job experience.

The following is a list of various situations in which you may find yourself.

1. If your education is pertinent to the position you are pursuing (i.e. a masters' degree, a doctorate, an education certification), then list it in reverse chronological order before you state your experience or skills. For example,

> Butler University, Indianapolis, Indiana
> Master of Business Administration, 1990
>
> DePauw University, Greencastle, Indiana
> Bachelor of Arts in Economics, 1985

2. If your education is not pertinent to the position you are pursuing BUT it is a degree of higher education AND you have under fifteen years of experience, then we suggest that you list it before you state your work experience or functional skills.

3. If you have more than fifteen years of experience AND your degree is not directly relevant to the position you seek, you will want to list your education toward the end of your resume.

4. If you are a recent high school graduate OR a recent college graduate, you will want to list the high school you attended, the city and the year you graduated. For example,

> North Central High School, 1985
> Indianapolis, Indiana

5. If you attended college BUT did not graduate, you will want to list the college and city, but do not list the date you would have graduated or the degree you would have received. It is acceptable to list your major or emphasis in school.

> Indiana University, Bloomington, Indiana
> Major: Computer Science

Activities and Professional Affiliations

Listing irrelevant hobbies and organizational affiliations can actually backfire. "Why would I care that he plays tournament chess?" "Anybody who goes skydiving is too big a risktaker!" "If she belongs to that organization, she may be a wild-eyed liberal!" On the other hand, well-chosen listings can demonstrate you are a well-rounded person, a person involved in your community, or a person advancing career knowledge outside the workplace.

Again, be aware of potential reaction and ask for input from objective advisors. As a guideline, list interests and affiliations only if they meet at least three of these criteria:

- You have been a member of this organization within the past five years.
- You are/were an active member.
- The organization relates to your career choice.
- The activity is generally held to be healthful, wholesome or otherwise positive.
- The activity will not offend or look silly to the reader.

Current or Previous Salaries

It is almost never advisable to list your salary demand on your resume. You risk sounding either overpriced or underpriced. You risk the reader jumping to conclusions about the salary level you would or would not accept—despite the fact their benefits may make a lower base salary very desirable. In general, it's best to negotiate salary further down the interviewing road.

If an application specifically requests salary history, you must use your cover letter to anticipate possible communication problems and deal with them. For example:

- "While my previous job was at a level of $_____, I am far more interested in a satisfying job than a specific income figure."
- "Frankly, I know I'm worth considerably more than my present income level and this confidence is the primary reason I'm interested in this position."
- "I hope we can discuss the income issue face-to-face. My previous employer did not offer some benefits which

your company makes available. I'm well aware these factors are just as important as monthly wages."

- "Within the past five years I have been earning between $30,000 and $33,000, in addition to various benefit programs. However, I would appreciate the opportunity to discuss with you a compensation plan relevant to the position of Brand Manager at XYZ Products, Inc."

References

At some point in the interviewing process, your references will become crucial. Most likely to be checked are professional references. Most interviewers assume your mother, pastor and close friends think well of you.

It is almost never necessary to include references on the resume. They take valuable space. And the interviewer will not need them until you've survived initial screening and, probably, an initial interview.

Many resumes simply state "References available upon request." As this is an obvious truth, it is equally acceptable to omit reference to references.

An exception to the above rule might be a professional reference of such weight that the opportunity to "name drop" might be helpful in grabbing the reader's attention. Examples would be widely known industry figures, public figures or critics.

Reasons for Leaving Previous or Current Positions

It is almost never advisable for your resume to list reasons for departing prior employment. These can be discussed during an interview. In some cases, they may be appropriate for discussion in your cover letter—but the resume should remain positive.

> **"It is almost never advisable to list your salary demand on your resume."**

Age, Race, Religion, Sex or National Origin

Equal Employment Opportunity laws state that it is illegal to hire, fire or refuse an interview for employment based on age, race, religion, sex or national origin. Thus, it is unnecessary to list those descriptions of yourself.

As a practical matter, many companies are attempting to balance their workforce to remedy past discrimination. If you are aware that a company is attempting to add more of whatever you are, you may be able to list affiliations, references to dates or other information which is informative but not blatant. This step is perfectly legal. The company could not ask you to list such information, but you are within the law to volunteer it.

Personal Information

Personal information is data such as height, weight, health status, marital status, number of children, names and ages of family members, and personal likes and dislikes. The resume industry is in major discord on this issue.

Obviously, the same anti-discrimination laws mentioned above preclude an employer from hiring based on most items of personal information. In fact, it is currently illegal for an interviewer to ask about a person's marital status, child count, and plans for having children.

For these reasons, it is increasingly acceptable to omit a personal section.

The same practical issue discussed previously is applicable. If you are applying for a job which would, for whatever reason, tilt toward someone who is 6'4" and weighs 220, then mention it. If you know that a company has a strong stance on family values, mention your family.

The PERSONAL section provides another opportunity for demonstration of your sense of humor. An Edge associate created a resume which was a real keeper with this personal section:

PERSONAL:

Height: 6'2"	Health: Excellent
Weight: 190 lbs.	Hat Size: 7
Single	Shoe Size: 11½
No Children	Tennis Shoe: Nike

Photographs

The advice concerning photographs is similar to the previous discussions. It is not necessary. It is certainly not common. It is risky in the sense that a reader might not "like your looks" for whatever reason. However, if some unique aspect of yourself is best communicated with a photograph, and if you (and your objective advisors) believe the photograph clearly gives you an Edge, it is acceptable.

When using a photograph, it is vital that print quality be excellent. Photo quality varies dramatically among printing processes and among printing companies. Be sure your company can do an excellent job.

One creative resume idea (almost over the Edge) was built around a head-to-foot photograph of an applicant with captions surrounding the photograph.

"Eyes that see the future with vision."

"Sleeves that are rolled up ready for hard work."

Endorsements

An endorsement is a quote from an associate or boss which describes your attributes or successes in a previous or current job. The endorsement is appropriate as part of a job description or functional skill description. An example of an endorsement follows.

> Facilitated week-long courses on substance abuse prevention. Spoke before numerous community groups on family mental health issues. Excellent ability to entertain the audience, while educating them on important topics of concern.
> *(bosses name, company)*

Using one or two endorsements if space allows can enhance your resume. Using more than two endorsements can make you or your resume appear self-exalting.

Resume Length

The length of your resume involves these considerations:

• Other things being equal, it is best that your resume not

exceed one page. This guideline is simply a bow to the reality that attention is hard to get. And attention to a lengthy resume is not likely. Desktop publishing technology which allows easy change of type styles and type sizes helps fit more information on a single page.

- However, if your career spans 20+ years or you are applying for very high level positions, it is arguable that you SHOULD have accumulated too much experience to fit onto a single page. In this case, work hard to create SUMMARIES and other attention-grabbing devices which inspire your reader to wade through the longer resume.

If your resume should fit one page but presently doesn't, you need an editor (yourself or your objective advisor):

- Is some of the information just plain irrelevant?
- Can some of the early job positions be eliminated or combined since they're not as meaningful as more recent information?
- Can some of your verbiage be trimmed of fat?
- Can you use a different format which doesn't waste as much space on the paper? For example, immense space is wasted by the age-old format of blocking text at the right and putting the single words EXPERIENCE or EDUCATION at the left.

"Mr. Smedley, if you're judging resumes on a per pound basis, here's your man!"

How Many Different Resumes Do I Need?

Even though elimination of multiple OBJECTIVES offers a way to reduce the number of resumes you need, it is generally accepted that Job Market 90s demands more than one version of your resume.

One successful Edge associate interviewed for marketing and public relations' positions by use of a functional resume with different emphasis on his skills. Another associate used a functional resume to apply for positions outside his immediate industry and a chronological resume to apply within his industry.

Certainly in the Edge strategy, you should consider resumes which are much less traditional when you know your odds of consideration are slim unless you dare to be different.

Other Resume Writing Books

Krannich, Ronald L., Ph.D. and William J. Banis., *High Impact Resumes and Letters: How To Communicate Your Qualifications To Employers.* Impact Publications, 9104-N Manassas Dr., Manassas Park, VA 22111. 1992.

Tepper, Ron., *Power Resumes.* John Wiley & Sons, Inc., 605 Third Ave., New York, NY 10158. 1992.

Yate, Martin John., *Resumes That Knock 'Em Dead.* Bob Adams, Inc., 260 Center St., Holbrook, MA 02343.

The Interview

Although the scope of this book does not include in-depth coverage of the interviewing process, it is too important to omit. (To successfully chase interviews without being fully prepared for those interviews seems akin to the dog who chases cars. What in the world does he do with it if he catches it?)

This chapter covers some fundamentals of the interviewing process and provides references for additional study and preparation.

Some have asked whether we feel the Edge concept of "daring to be different" should be stretched into the interviewing process. These would seem to be the key considerations:

- If your Edge resume has allowed you to survive a major screening process and you have reason to believe you are very competitive in terms of qualifications, personal traits and interviewing technique, it seems unduly risky to adopt unconventional interviewing tactics.

- If your Edge resume has allowed you to secure an interview against heavy odds (and this happens frequently), you face the same dilemma in the interviewing process that you faced with the resume. The competitors are likely to have a "better pedigree" in terms of direct

❝To successfully chase interviews without being fully prepared for those interviews seems akin to the dog who chases cars. What in the world does he do with it if he catches it?❞

experience. It makes no sense to ignore the likely disadvantage you face. Therefore, your interview must directly, skillfully address your likely shortcomings. Examples of appropriate comments might be:

- "I believe experience is important, certainly a person must be well-grounded in the fundamentals of our business. But there are people with so much experience that they've quit questioning, quit learning, quit growing. I feel fully ready to take on this job—and I'll be the kind of person who will never stand still. I'll grow as much as it's possible to grow in the job—and I'll look forward to whatever other positions the company allows me to tackle."

- "I am confident I have all the technical skills it takes to handle this job. And I'll bring the kind of positive attitude, enthusiasm and work ethic which can really help energize my department. When I was at Acme, I was able to generate a 12% increase in productivity—partly because I implemented new systems but mainly because I

"John, do you really think he's tough enough for a good practice interview?"

instilled a 'roll up your sleeves and get the job done' attitude which turned my department around."

- "I suppose there will be a few technical things I won't know the day I start—but I sure won't stand around feeling stupid. I am an aggressive learner. I find the people who know answers and I learn from them. I find the right books and articles, take the right courses. In other words, within days, not weeks, I'll be fully informed in every aspect of that position. And I'll keep growing from there!"

It is vitally important that the interviewing style be totally comfortable—the "real you" rather than an attempt to play a role. Therefore, whether the approach is rather conservative or more aggressive, it must fit your personality. At the same time, it's vital to...

Practice, Practice, Practice

It is a strange twist of human nature that we will spend significant time in rehearsal for minor speeches to minor organizations but we tend to "wing it" when it comes to job interviews.

In fact, for most of us, becoming comfortable in the interviewing process requires a great deal of practice.

One excellent technique is asking a friend to play interviewer to your interviewee. Request tough questions in random order. If possible, videotape your performance to watch for verbal slips (uh, um, ya know, uh, um) and any unpleasant nervous habits.

Of course, real interviews are the best practice—and the more you do the better. If possible, be like the young boy who asked a hostile girl to the dance. "Tom, why did you ask Nancy? You knew she'd say no." "I know, but I wanted to practice my asking so Melissa might say yes." A couple practice interviews for jobs you don't really want can be ideal practice for the really crucial interview.

The Library (again)

By now the map of your library is probably permanently etched on your brain. As we discussed in Chapter 7: Finding Opportunities, it is vital that you go into an interview with as much specific knowledge about the company as possible. Read, take notes, study! In addition to answering questions, you'll probably be asked to ask some. Here are some good general questions:

- *What are the day-to-day responsibilities of the person in this position?*
- *Why is this position open? Where is the person now who was previously in this position?*
- *What is a potential career path beginning with this position in the company?*
- *Exactly where does this position fit into the overall organizational structure of the company?*
- *Are there important changes such as expansion of products or services which will affect my position?*
- *Are the procedures of the position set in stone or is a person encouraged to contribute innovative new ideas?*

Asking questions such as these will serve to impress the interviewer as well as provide you with valuable information. Be aware, however, of a possible hidden agenda when an interviewer asks for your questions: if a set of questions are simplistic, it tips the interviewer that a person is very green or very unfamiliar with basic information about the company or industry.

Also, be aware that initiating conversation regarding salary and benefits during the first interview could harm your chances for a second interview. Some interviewers feel that early discussion of money is a clue that a person is focused on "what's in it for me?" rather than being a dedicated professional.

Some Interviewing Fundamentals

The time is now and you have arrived at your interview destination ten to fifteen minutes early. You've allowed the extra time to insure against traffic problems and to give yourself a few minutes in the restroom to be sure everything is groomed, tucked in and zipped. Your dress is conservative; appropriate as best you understand it for the kind of job for which you're applying. You have attended to the small details which some interviewers study carefully: shoes polished, nails in good shape, cologne/aftershave modest or non-existent.

Since you may be meeting with more than one interviewer, you've brought along several extra EDGE resumes. You have pen, paper and calculator in an impressive case or binder. You are prepared to complete an application form, having relevant dates of education, employment and military service. You have names, addresses and phone numbers of previous employers and references.

The interview begins:
You have taken whatever steps you take to overcome the biggest enemy: nervousness. Being relaxed is doubly crucial:
- A nervous candidate obviously does not exude the confidence people seek in an employee;
- Even worse, nervousness can shut down the mind and affect the voice—not the desired physical response for good interviewing.

Here are some concepts which may help you relax:
- Excellent preparation is critical. If you have studied the company, know more about the situation than competitive candidates, and have practiced your questions and answers, you can relax with the knowledge that you're well out in front of most applicants.

"You've allowed the extra time to insure against traffic problems and...to be sure everything is groomed, tucked in and zipped."

- The interviewer is just another human. In fact, many interviewers are uncomfortable with the process and are hopeful that there will be a "click" between personalities which will make the interview more pleasant. If it can be done gracefully, try to find some pre-interview bonding topics: kids, family, vacations and college experience to create a more pleasant relationship. Scanning the walls and desks for pictures, diplomas, or trip momentos may give clues. Generating a laugh can help, but joking is risky until you have a clue the interviewer has a sense of humor. If so, you can probably generate a thawing chuckle with lines such as:
  —"Do you mind if I sit over there (his chair)? I hate this side of the desk."
  —"It must be grim interviewing a bunch of people. Do you ever want to record your questions and just go golfing?"

Remember these basics:
- Eye contact is crucial. Many applicants sink from sight because poor eye contact makes them seem shifty.
- Answers should be kept under two minutes each. Be very sensitive to clues you are talking too much. Some interviewers begin fidgeting, glancing around the room, or watching their watches. Some might yawn. In the worst example we've ever heard, one applicant reported that his interviewer actually dozed off.
- Exaggeration is risky. Good interviewers make mental or written notes and often check references to verify answers.
- On the other hand, amplify answers to include information which sells your skills and accomplishments. For example, in response to a question about the number of people you've managed at one time, "As Sales Manager at ABC Products, I was responsible for hiring, training and managing as many as 15 sales representatives covering 4 states. My team exceeded quota by 75% during the three years I was there, so I feel my approach to management and motivation was very effective."
- Avoid speaking negatively about anything, particularly

your previous position, company or boss. Many interviewers are simply turned off by negatives. Others will conclude that the negatives are a clue that the applicant is a griper and complainer.

- Be sure to ask the interviewer what the next set of steps will be. His answer will probably give a strong clue regarding your status after the interview. "Well, uh, someone will be in touch" is much less promising than "We'll conduct follow-up interviews next week and I expect you'll be contacted."

- Follow-up the interview with a letter or hand-written thank you note which ties to the balance of the application process. "Thanks for the opportunity to meet with you. I'm looking forward to meeting with Mr. Sandifer next week. I'm more convinced than ever that this position represents an excellent career step and I'm hopeful you agree that my qualifications fit your requirements..."

Additional References

These references have been utilized by many Edge associates:

Hellman, Paul., *Ready, Aim, You're Hired! How to Job-Interview Successfully Anytime, Anywhere With Anyone.* AMACOM, New York, NY. 1986.

Medley, H. Anthony., *Sweaty Palms: The Neglected Art Of Being Interviewed.* Ten Speed Press, Box 7123, Berkeley, CA 94707. 1992.

Marcus, John J., *The Complete Job Interview Handbook.* Harper & Row Publishers, New York, NY 10022. 1988, 1985.

Yate, Martin J., *Knock 'Em Dead With Great Answers To Tough Interview Questions.* Bob Adams, Holbrook, MA 02343. 1992, 1991, 1990, 1988, 1987.

Interview Questions You May Be Asked

1. Tell me about yourself.
2. Why should I hire you?
3. Why are you looking for a new job?
4. Why did you leave your previous position?
5. Have you ever been fired from a job? Why?
6. What did you like most about your previous position?
7. What did you like least about your previous position?
8. Why do you want this position?
9. What other positions are you interviewing for?
10. What do you want from a job?
11. How would you describe the ideal job?
12. Why did you choose this career path?
13. What are your greatest strengths? Greatest weaknesses?
14. Where do you see yourself five years from now? Ten years from now?
15. What are some of your short-term goals?
16. What are some of your long-term goals?
17. Tell me about a goal you set for yourself recently and how you accomplished it.
18. What two or three accomplishments have given you the most satisfaction?
19. How do you determine or evaluate success?
20. What is the worst mistake you have ever made on the job? How did you remedy the problem?
21. What is a major problem that you have encountered and how did you deal with it?
22. What have you learned from your mistakes?
23. What motivates you?
24. How do you go about making important decisions?
25. If you could change something about your life, what would it be?
26. What activities are you involved in? What are your hobbies?
27. What have you learned from participation in activities away from your job/career?

28. What is the last book you read? What is the last movie you saw?

29. What do you know about this company?

30. What do you think a company should provide its employees?

31. What criteria are you using to evaluate the company you hope to work for?

32. What do you think it takes to be successful in a company like ours?

33. In what ways do you think you can make a contribution to our company?

34. What qualities should a successful manager possess?

35. Tell me about the best boss you ever had. The worst.

36. How well do you work under pressure?

37. How do you think a friend who knows you well would describe you? How do you think a former associate/colleague would describe you?

38. What is your best friend like? What does he or she do?

39. Do you consider yourself a leader or a follower? Why?

40. Do you prefer working with others or by yourself? Why?

41. What type of personality is the most difficult for you to get along with?

42. Why did you choose the college you attended?

43. Why didn't you attend college?

44. How and why did you choose your major?

45. What college subjects did you like best? Why?

46. How was your college education funded?

47. How many days of work did you miss in your last position?

48. How long do you plan on staying in your next position?

49. How do you feel about travel? Locally? Nationally? Internationally? How many days out of the year are acceptable?

50. How do you feel about relocation?

51. Has anyone made you an offer yet? If so, why haven't you accepted? If not, why not?

52. What are you currently earning?

53. How much do you feel you are worth? How much do you want to be earning?

Step by Step Action Plan

E ffectively executing the Edge strategy requires careful organization of a job search campaign. This requires more work than the notion of randomly mailing resumes and hoping for the best. It is also much more effective.

It's important to carefully organize the components of your campaign. The following pages provide forms which may be helpful. You are free to reproduce these forms or to modify the designs to better fit your needs.

The forms include:

- An overall master plan including target and actual timetable.
- A research form for logging information about individual companies.
- A networking form for logging contacts and leads.
- A marketing form for logging your outgoing mailings.
- An interview form for detailing progress with companies who have responded to your initial contact.

These thumbnails show sample uses of each form:

This form may be photocopied for personal use. May not be resold.

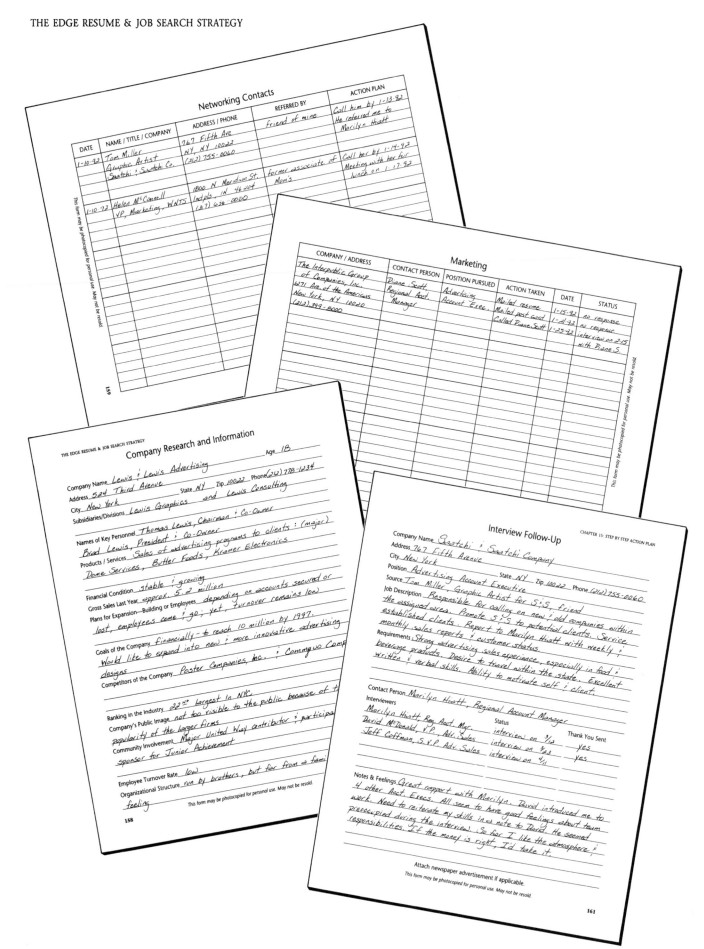

Networking Contacts

DATE	NAME / TITLE / COMPANY	ADDRESS / PHONE	REFERRED BY	ACTION PLAN
1-10-92	Tom Miller, Graphic Artist, Saatchi & Saatchi Co.	767 Fifth Ave, NY, NY 10022, (212) 755-0060	Friend of mine	Call him by 1-13-92. He referred me to Marilyn Hiatt
1-10-92	Helen McConnell, VP, Marketing, WNTS	1800 N. Meridian St., Indpls, IN 46204, (317) 636-0000	Former associate of Mom's	Call her by 1-14-92. Meeting with her for lunch on 1-17-92

159

Marketing

COMPANY / ADDRESS	CONTACT PERSON	POSITION PURSUED	ACTION TAKEN	DATE	STATUS
The Interpublic Group of Companies, Inc., 1271 Ave. of the Americas, New York, NY 10020, (212) 399-8000	Diane Scott, Regional Acct. Manager	Advertising Account Exec.	Mailed resume	1-15-92	no response
			Mailed post card	1-21-92	no response
			Called Diane Scott	1-25-92	interview on 2-15 with Diane S.

Company Research and Information

Age _1B_

Company Name _Lewis & Lewis Advertising_
Address _524 Third Avenue_
City _New York_ State _NY_ Zip _10022_ Phone _(212) 778-1234_
Subsidiaries/Divisions _Lewis Graphics and Lewis Consulting_

Names of Key Personnel _Thomas Lewis, Chairman & Co-Owner_
Brad Lewis, President & Co-Owner
Products / Services _Sales of advertising programs to clients: (major)_
Dome Services, Butter Foods, Kramer Electronics

Financial Condition _stable & growing_
Gross Sales Last Year _approx. 5.2 million_
Plans for Expansion—Building or Employees _depending on accounts secured or_
lost, employees come & go; yet, turnover remains low
Goals of the Company _financially - to reach 10 million by 1997._
Would like to expand into new & more innovative advertising
designs
Competitors of the Company _Poster Companies, Inc., & Commquo Comp_

Ranking in the Industry _22nd largest in NYC._
Company's Public Image _not too visible to the public because of t_
popularity of the larger firms
Community Involvement _Major United Way contributor & participa_
sponsor for Junior Achievement

Employee Turnover Rate _low_
Organizational Structure _run by brothers, but far from a fami_
feeling

This form may be photocopied for personal use. May not be resold.

158

Interview Follow-Up

Company Name _Saatchi & Saatchi Company_
Address _767 Fifth Avenue_
City _New York_ State _NY_ Zip _10022_ Phone _(212) 755-0060_
Position _Advertising Account Executive_
Source _Tom Miller, Graphic Artist for S&S, friend_
Job Description _Responsible for calling on new & old companies within_
the assigned area. Promote S&S to potential clients. Service
established clients. Report to Marilyn Hiatt with weekly &
monthly sales reports & customer status.
Requirements _Strong advertising sales experience, especially in food &_
beverage products. Desire to travel within the state. Excellent
written & verbal skills. Ability to motivate self & clients.

Contact Person _Marilyn Hiatt, Regional Account Manager_
Interviewers

Interviewers	Status	Thank You Sent
Marilyn Hiatt Reg. Acct. Mgr.	interview on 3/12	
David McDonald, V.P., Adv. Sales	interview on 3/23	yes
Jeff Coffman, S.V.P. Adv. Sales	interview on 4/11	yes

Notes & Feelings _Great rapport with Marilyn. David introduced me to_
4 other Acct. Execs. All seem to have good feelings about team
work. Need to reiterate my skills in a note to David. He seemed
preoccupied during the interview. So far I like the atmosphere &
responsibilities. If the money is right, I'd take it.

Attach newspaper advertisement if applicable.
This form may be photocopied for personal use. May not be resold.

161

Edge Job Campaign

	PLAN	DEADLINE	✔ COMPLETED
Preplanning & Research			
Networking			
Prospecting & Finding Opportunity			
Resume Preparation	Writing		
	Design		
	Estimates		
	Produced		
Other Campaign Elements			

This form may be photocopied for personal use. May not be resold.

Company Research and Information

Company Name_____ Age_____

Address_____

City_____ State_____ Zip_____ Phone_____

Subsidiaries/Divisions_____

_____

Names of Key Personnel_____

_____

Products / Services_____

_____

_____

Financial Condition_____

Gross Sales Last Year_____

Plans for Expansion—Building or Employees_____

_____

_____

Goals of the Company_____

_____

_____

Competitors of the Company_____

_____

_____

Ranking in the Industry_____

Company's Public Image_____

_____

Community Involvement_____

_____

_____

Employee Turnover Rate_____

Organizational Structure_____

_____

This form may be photocopied for personal use. May not be resold.

Networking Contacts

DATE	NAME / TITLE / COMPANY	ADDRESS / PHONE	REFERRED BY	ACTION PLAN

This form may be photocopied for personal use. May not be resold.

COMPANY / ADDRESS	CONTACT PERSON	POSITION PURSUED	ACTION TAKEN	DATE	STATUS

Marketing

This form may be photocopied for personal use. May not be resold.

Interview Follow-Up

Company Name_____

Address_____

City_____ State_____ Zip_____ Phone_____

Position_____

Source_____

Job Description _____

_____

_____

_____

Requirements_____

_____

_____

_____

_____

Contact Person_____

Interviewers	Status	Thank You Sent
_____	_____	_____
_____	_____	_____
_____	_____	_____
_____	_____	_____
_____	_____	_____

Notes & Feelings_____

_____

_____

_____

_____

_____

_____

Attach newspaper advertisement if applicable.

This form may be photocopied for personal use. May not be resold.

Executing Edge Designs

This section will cover the process of actually creating your Edge resume. We'll be referring to specific samples, using the page number on each printed sample in Chapter 10. We'll give insight into the printing processes including the bold step of giving some likely ranges of cost. For most designs the cost for 250 copies is very close to the cost for fewer copies. Running an additional 250 would be substantially less than the first 250. Be aware that costs vary significantly in different parts of the country and among printers in the same part of the country. Ask for complete estimates before placing your actual order.

The type for every sample was created on a basic desktop publishing system. In general, execution of Edge resumes DOES NOT require typesetting techniques more sophisticated than standard desktop publishing. This means you can actually separate the process into two steps:

1. Develop and execute a unique design (which we'll call the "shell").

2. Use your own desktop system or work with a local resume consultant to create the set of words which are printed into the shell.

The designs shown in Chapter 10 utilize five elements of printing technology:

1. Paper Selection:
A feeling of excellent quality requires far more than

"For those struggling with budget considerations, it is helpful to know that real graphic impact can be made without significant cost."

20# copier paper. Fortunately, upgrading paper is relatively inexpensive. If you purchase paper through your printer, the "upcharge" for each sheet of 8.5x11 stock should be 3-5¢ versus 20# bond. The upcharge for premium envelopes will be in the 8-10¢ range. Therefore, utilizing high quality paper for a package consisting of a cover letter, a resume and an envelope should be approximately $20 per hundred more than utilizing cheap paper.

For some positions, use of recycled paper can show your awareness of a significant social issue. The sample on page 67, for example, is printed on recycled stock and the recycled symbol is printed on the resume. Art for this symbol is included in Appendix B.

2. Use of Non-black Ink:

To a remarkable extent, traditional resumes utilize black ink, black laser toner, or black copier powder. The first step toward a stand-out resume can be accomplished by the simple technique of putting non-black colors on the page. Some of the printing techniques are sophisticated. You learned others in kindergarten. And for those struggling with budget considerations, it is helpful to know that real graphic impact can be made without significant cost.

• It is possible to color a part of your resume with felt-tip markers. This is a zero-cost alternative but can be extremely effective. The post-it note shown on page 61, the highlighting on page 63, the apple on page 65, and the gull/eagle on page 69 could be easily colored by hand. Even the monogram on page 97 or the chart on page 101 could be hand-done. Hand-coloring is as simple as printing a "hollow" design using a copier or quick printing process (i.e. the outline of a monogram letter), then staying inside the lines.

• Color copier technology offers the second most economical approach to achieving non-black resumes. At its simplest, the entire resume can be done using a non-black toner. More interesting is to create multi-color resumes by successively copying different parts of the resume in different colors. Resumes on pages 67 and 71 offer examples which can be easily executed using a color copier.

- Quick print multi-color printing. Most quick print shops utilize small offset presses which can be changed-over to any ink color. Quick printers typically charge $25 to "wash up" a press, after which the cost of 2-color printing is about twice the cost of one color. This technology is ideal for designs too intricate to handle on a copier, yet simple enough that they do not require heavy ink coverage or absolutely perfect alignment of the various colors. Quick printing would be appropriate for most of our two-color Edge designs.

- Commercial printing. Commercial printers have larger, more precise presses which can execute jobs such as the resume on page 79—a "full-reverse" which requires even coverage of the entire printed page. Edge samples on pages 51, 87, 89, 91, 93 and 95 utilize "4-color process" printing, often done by commercial printers but within the capability of sophisticated quick printers. Original 4-color printing involves a cost of several hundred dollars. A far more economical approach to 4-color resumes is the purchase of "pre-printed" shells. This is discussed in Appendix C.

3. Foiling:

Resumes on pages 57, 69, 81, 83, 85, 89, 97, 99, 103 and 107 utilize metallic foil. Most printers do not do foiling "in house," rather sending that portion of the job to companies which specialize in foil. The process is expensive, probably involving an initial charge in the range of $50 and perhaps 10-15¢ per foiled piece.

An important note regarding foiling: if cover letters or resumes will be printed in laser printers, the heat of this process may melt the foil. It is best to do finish foil resumes through offset printing and to avoid foil on cover letters if laser technology will be used.

4. Diecutting:

The process of cutting out part of the paper or creating unique shapes involves diecutting. Resumes on pages 49, 53, 55, 57, 101 and 105 utilize diecutting. The approximate cost to diecut is $30-50 for a new die, $30-50 to set up the machinery, and $3-5 per hundred diecut pieces.

Like foiling, this process is typically handled by specialty companies.

5. Use of Varying Paper Sizes:

The traditional resume is 8.5x11. A popular alternative, particularly for those with longer resumes, is 11x17. This format provides 4-sides of 8.5x11 pages. The examples on pages 53-56 use an 11x17 sheet (plus diecutting). The resumes on pages 73-76 utilize the idea of a completely different size. In Chapter 13 we discuss the gimmick of an oversize resume, 17x22. A jumbo resume would be relatively expensive, probably $200+, and would need to be run in a commercial company having large presses.

6. Use of Different Formats:

The traditional resume, and most Edge designs, have the 8.5" edge "up." The sample on page 87 shows an alternate format.

Specifications of our Samples:

These specifications could be discussed with your printer or advisor. He may offer suggestions on modifications which will allow fully acceptable alternatives to be created. This is particularly true of paper choice, but the samples may also trigger new design ideas.

Page 49
Cover letter with diecut puzzle piece to match page 51.
Paper: Cross Pointe Passport, 28 lb. script with laser finish
Color: Pumice
Inks: Black
Techniques: Diecut puzzle piece; however, the concept also works if only the outline is printed, contrasting with the "colored in" piece on page 51.
Art Preparation: Art requires outline of a puzzle piece. Usable art is included in Appendix B. Or any puzzle piece of your choice can be outlined.
Estimated cost for 250: $150.00*
Preprints: Shell available through The Edge.*
Other Considerations: Be sure a diecut piece of paper will work in the printer doing your cover letters.

Page 51
Resume with printed puzzle piece to match cover letter, on page 49.
Paper: Cross Pointe Passport, 28 lb. script with laser finish.
Color: Pumice
Inks: 4-color process
Techniques: Design can also work using one non-black color for puzzle piece.
Art Preparation: In 1-color printing, the printer needs only a "filled in" puzzle piece to shoot. For 4-color art, an actual puzzle piece can be shot or color art can be created from any usable color pattern.
Estimated cost for 250: $450.00*
Preprints: Shell available through The Edge.*
Other Considerations: Be sure a diecut piece of paper will work in the printer doing your cover letters.

Cost estimates DO NOT assume use of preprinted shells. See Appendix C for discussion of the savings associated with preprints.

Pages 53 and 55
An 11x17.5 "folder," a single piece of paper having these features:
3. Simulated cover letter being held to the front of the folder with a simulated paper clip (actually all printed).
4. Other side of the folder, featuring die cut tab for your name which will show outside a stack of traditional 8.5x11 resumes.
Important Note: to show this sample in the book, we sized it so the tab fits inside the book. However, the real-life version should be large enough that the tab extends past 8.5x11. This can be accomplished by using 11x17.5" stock or by using 11x17" stock and "shortfolding" the front at about 8" so the tab side is 9"
Paper: Hammermill 70 lb. offset.
Color: Ivory
Inks: Black
Techniques: Diecut folder tab. The design concept of the simulated cover letter is unique enough that the tab element can be eliminated. Printing can be handled by any quick printer able to handle the specified sheet size.
Art Preparation: Simulated paper clip is included in Appendix B.
Estimated cost for 250: $320.00*
Preprints: Diecut folders available through The Edge.*
Other Considerations: Cover letter is actually typed on the folded version of the resume. Must utilize conventional typewriter or friction-fed computer printer rather than a laser printer. Concept will also work with the cover letter (probably a smaller "monarch" size, typically about 7x10" actually paperclipped to the front of the folder. In this case, the front cover would include copy such as:

Resume
John A. Smith
111 East Ash Drive
Indianapolis, IN 46260
(317) 555-1212

Management—Operations
Cost Containment

Should be mailed in larger envelope, to avoid any additional folding.

Pages 57 and 59
Computer with diecut screen.
Paper: Gilbert Oxford 24 lb. bond.
Color: Sky
Inks: Black/silver foil
Techniques: Foiled computer with diecut screen which allows name, address and phone to show from resume.

Art Preparation: Art for computer is included in Appendix B.
Estimated cost for 250: $450.00*
Other Considerations: Test in advance whether your cover letter printer will handle a sheet with a hole in it. Also, choose a commercial printer able to do close register work because foiling and diecut positioning are critical. The idea of the opening would work for art as varied as an automobile, truck, or even a tree.

Page 61
Cover letter or resume with a simulated Post-It note.
Paper: Beckett Cambric 70 lb. linen.
Color: Arctic
Inks: Black/PMS 102.
Techniques: Simple 2-color printing. Yellow could be hand-colored.
Estimated cost for 250: $150.00*
Art Preparation: Art for Post-It note is included in Appendix B.
Other Considerations: Concept is gimmicky—assumptively writing the reader's message about your interview. Definitely close to "The Outer Edge." Can either print a message such as "Excellent Applicant—Definitely Interview" in simulated handwriting or can print the Post-It Note as a blank yellow section and write different messages tailored to different recipients. Might work best on cover letter so resume is more traditional.

Page 63
Traditional resume with yellow highlighting.
Paper: Beckett Cambric 70 lb. linen.
Color: Arctic
Inks: Black/PMS 102
Techniques: Simple 2-color printing. Yellow could be hand colored.
Estimated cost for 250: $150.00*
Art Preparation: Art for the highlighting section is simply black blobs, positioned correctly which can be printed in yellow over the traditional resume.
Other Considerations: Excellent method of highlighting specific elements of resume. Unusual, yet a recognized means of making things stand out on the page.

Page 65
Teacher's resume with apple and chalkboard.
Paper: Beckett Enhance 70 lb. text.
Color: Ultra White
Inks: Black/PMS 185/PMS 347.
Techniques: Can be copied and handcolored or printed by precise 3-color printing.
Art Preparation: Art usable for

apple and blackboard included in Appendix B. Words for blackboard can be created using desktop publishing reverse type.
Estimated cost for 250: $225.00*

Page 67
Teacher's resume with alphabet.
Paper: Hopper Proterra 70 lb. text
Color: Oyster
Inks: Black/PMS 312
Estimated cost for 250: $150.00*

Page 69
Resume with seagull.
Paper: Beckett Enhance 70 lb. text.
Color: Marble Blue
Inks: Black/gold foil.
Techniques: Sample shown is simple printing with a gold foiled seagull. A lower cost alternative could be achieved by printing an outline of the seagull and handcoloring.
Art Preparation: Seagull art is included in Appendix B.
Estimated cost for 250: $200.00*
Other Considerations: Concept of foiled art works for broad variety of symbols. Also works as two-color printing. Can use the same design for cover letter and resume. However, see our caution about foil and laser printers.

Page 71
Two-color emphasis of main elements.
Paper: Beckett Cambric 70 lb. linen.
Color: Marble
Inks: Black/PMS 215
Techniques: Simple 2-color printing; or can be done on color copier.
Estimated cost for 250: $150.00*

Pages 73-76
4-panel resume with unique size, approximately 11x13.
Paper: Beckett Enhance 70 lb. text.
Color: Marble Tan
Inks: PMS 470
Techniques: Simple 1-color printing, can be executed on quality color copier able to print larger than 8.5x11.
Estimated cost for 250: $250.00*
Other Considerations: Cover letter stock needs to be sized for compatibility. Should be mailed in larger envelope to avoid additional folds.

Page 77
Resume with world map—printed 2-sides.
Paper: Beckett Cambric 70 lb. linen
Color: Birch
Inks: PMS 470
Techniques: Simple 1-color printing.
Estimated cost for 250: $220.00*

Cost estimates DO NOT assume use of preprinted shells. See Appendix C for discussion of the savings associated with preprints.

Other Considerations: Should be folded so map shows on outside.

Page 79
Full-reverse resume.
Paper: Lynx 70 lb. offset smooth
Color: White
Inks: PMS 295
Techniques: Full reverse, printed on press large enough to evenly cover entire page.
Art Preparation: Art is traditional resume. Reverse is created by commercial printing techniques.
Estimated cost for 250: $200.00*
Other Considerations: Any ink color relevant to the position or career choice can be utilized.

Page 81
Traditional resume with color bar for emphasis.
Paper: Beckett Enhance 70 lb. text
Color: Frost
Inks: PMS 301/silver foil
Techniques: 1-color printing. Works best if printed on oversized stock for trim to bleed 3 sides and on a press large enough to evenly cover solid bar.
Estimated cost for 250: $220.00*

Page 83
Foiled header in color bar.
Paper: Beckett Cambric 70 lb. linen
Color: Marble
Inks: Black/PMS 215/gold foil
Techniques: 2-color printing plus foil. Works best if printed on oversize stock for trim to bleed 3 sides.
Estimated cost for 250: $300.00*

Page 85
Copper foiled penny.
Paper: Beckett Cambric 70 lb. linen
Color: Birch
Inks: Black/copper foil
Techniques: Simple print with copper foil.
Estimated cost for 250: $220.00*
Preprints: Shell available through The Edge.*

Page 87
Multi-color bar chart resume.
Paper: Cross Pointe Passport 28# Script with laser finish.
Color: Pumice
Inks: 4-color process.
Techniques: Commercial 4-color printing.
Art Preparation: From scratch, requires artist with high degree of knowledge of commercial printing.
Estimated cost for 250: $450.00*
Other Considerations: Cost can be reduced by use of "screened color." For example, the printing could be 2-

color, black and blue with each bar printed at a different screen percentage of the blue ink.

Page 89-95
4-color border stock. Resume on page 89 also features a foiled bar.
Paper: Gilbert Neu-tec 28 lb. bond.
Color: Ultra White
Inks: 4-color process; page 89 has gold foil
Techniques: Commercial 4-color printing
Art Preparation: Traditional printing inside color shell. If original art is to be prepared, should be done in consultation with a graphic artist familiar with process printing.
Estimated cost for 250: $450.00*
Preprints: Shells available through The Edge.*

Page 97
Foiled monogram.
Paper: Beckett Ridge 70# text
Color: Bamboo
Inks: Black with gold foil
Techniques: Simple printing with foiled initial.
Art Preparation: Usuable clip art for monogram included in Appendix B. Any appropriate letters can be used.

Estimated cost for 250: $220.00*
Other Considerations: Low cost alternative is printed letter in outline form and hand-coloring to make the letter non-black. A color letter could also be added by simple printing or color copying. Design can be used as both resume and cover letter. See caution regarding foiling and laser printers.

Page 99
Foiled computer disk.
Paper: Beckett Ridge 70# text
Color: Colonial White
Inks: Black/PMS 312/silver foil
Techniques: Precise 2-color printing plus foil.
Art Preparation: Clip art for disk presented in Appendix B.
Estimated cost for 250: $300.00*
Other Considerations: Can work for both resume and cover letter. See foiling caution.
Preprints: Shells available through The Edge.*

Page 101
Two-color graph.
Paper: Beckett Enhance 70 lb. text
Color: Ultra White
Inks: Black/PMS 320
Techniques: Precise 2-color printing.

Art Preparation: From scratch, requires artist with high degree of knowledge of commercial printing.
Estimated cost for 250: $150.00*
Preprints: Shell available through The Edge.*

Page 103
Foiled quoation marks for quote emphasis.
Paper: Hammermill Regalia 24 lb. writing.
Color: Olde Porcelain
Inks: Black/Pantone violet/gold foil.
Techniques: Simple 2-color printing plus foil.
Estimated cost for 250: $300.00*
Other Considerations: Quote can be pulled from the resume for emphasis, can be an endorsement, or can be a suitable "famous quotation."
Preprints: Shells available through The Edge.*

Page 105
Diecut telephone.
Paper: Cross Pointe Passport 80# felt
Color: Coral Sand
Inks: Warm Grey 9
Techniques: Simple 1-color printing with diecut to outline phone.
Estimated cost for 250: $150.00*
Other Considerations: A range of shapes can be diecut.
Preprints: Shells available through The Edge.*

Page 107
Foiled dollar sign.
Paper: Hopper Skytone 60 lb. text
Color: Sage
Inks: Black/PMS 340/gold foil
Techniques: Simple 2-color printing plus foil.
Art Preparation: Clip art for dollar sign included in Appendix B.
Estimated cost for 250: $300.00*
Other Considerations: Can work for both resume and cover letter. See foiling caution.
Preprints: Shells available through The Edge.*

Cost estimates DO NOT assume use of preprinted shells. See Appendix C for discussion of the savings associated with preprints.

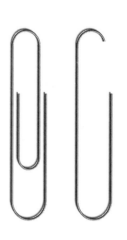

Clip Art

Many Edge designs include graphic art. This section provides art which may be helpful in preparation of your resume/cover letter. If you are skilled in preparing art, the process of calculating proper size, making reductions or enlargements and pasting the art will make sense. If you are utilizing professional help in your design, this section will make sense to your professional.

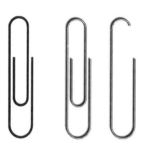

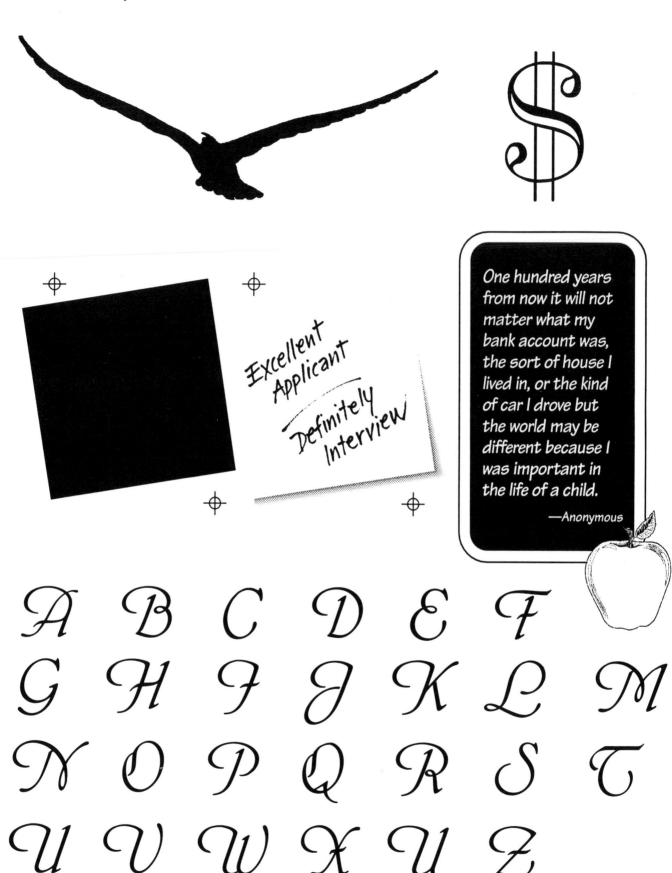

Excellent
Applicant

Definitely
Interview

One hundred years
from now it will not
matter what my
bank account was,
the sort of house I
lived in, or the kind
of car I drove but
the world may be
different because I
was important in
the life of a child.

—Anonymous

$\mathcal{A}$ $\mathcal{B}$ $\mathcal{C}$ $\mathcal{D}$ $\mathcal{E}$ $\mathcal{F}$

$\mathcal{G}$ $\mathcal{H}$ $\mathcal{I}$ $\mathcal{J}$ $\mathcal{K}$ $\mathcal{L}$ $\mathcal{M}$

$\mathcal{N}$ $\mathcal{O}$ $\mathcal{P}$ $\mathcal{Q}$ $\mathcal{R}$ $\mathcal{S}$ $\mathcal{T}$

$\mathcal{U}$ $\mathcal{V}$ $\mathcal{W}$ $\mathcal{X}$ $\mathcal{Y}$ $\mathcal{Z}$

Resume Shells

As indicated in Appendix A, costs of unique resumes can vary significantly. A complex, custom-designed resume can cost several hundred dollars. If affordable, the benefit is likely to justify this cost. However, for many job-seekers, budget is a key consideration.

The "shell" provides a cost-reduction alternative. You purchase paper which has already received the graphic treatment which will make the resume unusual. As an example, review the samples on pages 49 and 51, utilizing a missing puzzle piece for the cover letter and a printed puzzle piece for the resume. Your shell package consists of (1) blank paper with a diecut hole on which you type your own cover letter; (2) paper with the puzzle piece printed on which you print or copy your resume; and (3) matching envelopes.

The Edge is one source of preprinted shells. For information, write or call:

The Edge Resume and Job Search Strategy
350 Gradle Drive
Carmel, Indiana 46032-7536
317-573-0234
FAX 317-573-0239